Pascal Hügli | Yonghan Lee | Richard Dettling

IGNORE AT YOUR OWN RISK

The New Decentralized World of Bitcoin and Blockchain

ISBN 978-3-9525108-1-0

For questions and suggestions:
contact@kryptobu.ch

Based on the original book in German "Ignorieren auf eigene Gefahr"

Cover design: Fabian Widmer
Cover picture: Richard Dettling
Proofreading: DoEun Kwon
Comic: «The Bankey»
Print on Demand, Amazon

First edition: November 2019

www.kryptobu.ch

To our wives and children

Table of Contents

Acknowledgments

Dmitrij Gawrisch and DoEun Kwon for the inspiring proofreading. Daniel Jungen as a sparring partner. Fabian Widmer and Joel Walser for the graphically trained eye. Supporters for the financial contribution. The whole crypto community for feedback and help. And Satoshi Nakamoto for creating Bitcoin at a time when it is needed more than ever.

Preface

Dear reader, instead of letting the dangerous-sounding title of this book scare you away, you pushed the door wide open into the crypto world. Way to go! I can promise you that you will not regret this step.

As you will learn on the following pages, Bitcoin, blockchain technology and cryptoassets combine ideas and insights from economics, mathematics, computer science, philosophy and psychology. So, as you can imagine, they involve highly complex and intellectual concepts. But it is precisely this interdisciplinary approach that opens up fascinating nexuses and stimulates the mind. Trust me, I speak from experience.

The path of knowledge leads through monetary and economic history, solves cryptographic riddles, studies game theory incentives, puts well-known institutions to the acid test, ponders the fundamental nature of things and much more. As with all groundbreaking innovations, crypto raises fundamental questions: Can a digital collection of zeros and ones have value and be exchanged for goods? Can non-state private money even exist? Why is human trust a security risk? Why is today's financial system not socially scalable enough?

These and many other questions were hardly seriously discussed before the arrival of cryptoassets. Because the established system seemed to have no real alternative—except perhaps for hardcore Marxists or anarcho-capitalists, nobody dared to question it in principle. But Bitcoin, as the very first cryptoasset, has changed that. In order to comprehend and utilize its revolutionary power, we must broaden our horizons to include theories that mainstream thinking has often not even heard of.

The reading of this book is therefore an eye-opening experience in many respects. In addition to intellectual curiosity, it will demand openness of thought and perseverance. For this, dear reader, you will be rewarded generously with new and fascinating insights—and you will also have a lot of fun along the way. This is not least due to the entertaining comics by Yonghan Lee and Richard Dettling, who interpret the history of the crypto world in a very unique way. At the beginning of each chapter, you will find a comic that is rather independent of the chapter itself. Altogether, the comics tell the fictional story of a journalist named Kali and a developer named Jay, who dive into the decentralized crypto world with the help of the digital oracle Eva. On their journey, they meet well-known personalities in the cryptoscene, who explain the new technology, as well as its advantages and pitfalls. The more Kali and Jay learn about Bitcoin, Ethereum and blockchain technology, the more enthusiastic they become. Much to the annoyance of Lord IB of Kratz and Herbert, who fight the up-and-coming crypto movement using all means. Until it comes to the showdown…

As you will soon see, you can easily get lost in the crypto world. I have experienced this myself on countless occasions. It is a never-ending rabbit hole. If you haven't entered it yet, you should do it right now. I'm firmly convinced that those who have not yet paid any attention to the topic of Bitcoin, blockchains and cryptoassets and continue to do so run the risk of missing out on one of the most exciting developments of our time.

The development of cryptoassets and decentralized blockchains is still in its infancy. So the train hasn't left yet, but you should get on now so you don't miss it. Not only will you be able to join in the conversation when the topic of Bitcoin comes up at the dinner table, but you'll also be able to help shape this new decentralized world. Or even earn money with it—in times of zero and negative interest rates, cryptoassets can ultimately be lucrative investments.

Like all revolutionaries, crypto enthusiasts tend to exaggerate the new and demonize the former—in this case, the financial and economic system that is perceived as unfair and immoral. Even this book, which strives for an objective and just point of view, will not be immune to this at every point and, in cases of doubt, speak out in favor of crypto. However, in the realm of crypto developments, ideas and criticisms do not simply remain theoretical—the new decentralized world of Bitcoin offers a real alternative. It's still a big and great experiment though, which, to be fair, has yet to fulfill most of its promises.

I wish you a stimulating, enriching and, in every respect, life-changing read!

Pascal Hügli, July 2019

Introduction

On December 17, 2017, the crypto world was filled with excitement. On this third Sunday of the month, a week before Christmas, at exactly 14 hours and 4 minutes Central European Time, the price of the cryptocurrency bitcoin broke through the $20,000 USD mark for the first time. A year before, one bitcoin had cost only about $800 USD. It was truly a legendary ascent.

But then the saying "what goes up must come down" became a sobering reality. In the first few months of the new year, the price first fell slowly, then plummeted. On December 17, 2018, exactly 12 months later, it stood at only $3,300 USD. That was water to the mills of numerous pundits criticizing the crypto world. Many made fun of the cryptocurrency, cheerfully joking that there was an early Christmas sale of bitcoin going on. And even within the crypto community, many had no choice but to drown the great disillusionment in self-mockery.

Those who currently still deal with crypto often hear the question "Does this Bitcoin thing still exist?" And opponents and skeptics feel that they have been proven right about cryptocurrencies all along—for calling them a bubble, a snowball system, a construct for criminals and even an energy catastrophe in this time of climate change. Thus, critics concluded once and for all: it is pointless to pay attention to this "crypto thingy."

Harsh words are also leveled against Bitcoin from the official side. The Switzerland-based Bank for International Settlements, for example, has repeatedly expressed its severe viewpoint. "Overall, the decentralized technology of cryptocurrencies, however sophisticated, is a poor substitute for the solid institutional backing of money," wrote this bank for central banks in its annual report for 2018.

Financial specialists from traditional banks to monetary authorities, as well as famous economists such as Joseph Stiglitz, Jamie Dimon, Agustín Carstens and Nouriel Roubini, are pulling out all the stops to discredit Bitcoin. Vitor Constâncio, the vice president of the powerful European Central Bank (ECB), called Bitcoin "a kind of tulip" and compared it to the Dutch tulip mania, the mother of all speculative bubbles.

In the 17th century, greedy speculators of all social classes in the flourishing nation of Holland are said to have triggered a real buying frenzy for tulip bulbs. According to the popular story, more and more people—including many poor people—were infected by this hysteria, literally exchanging their last shirt for a tulip. Until the tulip bubble finally burst and ruined many people and the entire Dutch economy.

But this story has little in common with reality. As historian Anne Goldgar points out in her book *Tulipmania: Money, Honor, and Knowledge in the Dutch Golden Age*, the number of people affected by this tulip fever was actually rather negligible. It was mainly wealthy traders who bought and sold tulip bulbs. There is nothing in the archives to be found of chimney sweeps—the epitome of the lower classes—dealing with tulips.

The assertion that tulip bulbs changed owners hundreds of times, thus leading to ever higher prices, is also greatly exaggerated. As Goldgar found out, the longest retail chain consisted of just five people. The tulips often changed hands at the very price at which they had been bought.

And what about the bankruptcies that are said to have occurred on a massive scale in the course of the burst of the tulip bubble? Goldgar could not find a single instance in the archive documents. Although a lot has been written about losses and bad investments, the historian couldn't point out one tulip dealer who had ruined himself. The Dutch economy was also only weakly affected. Widespread collapse? No sign at all. Ever since Goldgar published her research, other historians have come to similar conclusions.

According to her, the fact that many economists today consider tulip mania to be the mother of all bubbles is due to the distribution of prominent flyers and propaganda by Dutch Calvinists. At that time, these influential guardians of morals condemned speculation in tulip bulbs as immoral because they disliked the dynamics of the Netherlands' economic ascent, and worried that such a boost of consumerism would lead to the decay of society.

These pamphlets later became the basis for historians reporting on this epoch of Dutch history. The most influential was Charles Mackay's popular book *Extraordinary Popular Delusions and the Madness of Crowds*. Over the years, the book has become an important source for information on the tulip hysteria and continues to be so to this day.

Similar to the Calvinists of that time, today's bankers, politicians and economic figureheads are on their way to go down in history as puritanical reactionaries. In doing so, they sometimes resemble the Luddites, who opposed change for fear of losing their livelihoods. But they could not and cannot stop progress. Technological and economic progress are often marked by euphoria and excess. Often a good idea is enough to get rich overnight. This, of course, brings out envy—sometimes one of the reasons why exponents of the "old" economy disrespect the new economy and its supporter. A frequently heard objection by bankers is that while they have to obey all kinds of law and regulations, crypto projects operate in a legal vacuum. But in the end, this opposition is also due to the fear of losing one's own privileges. As we will see in the course of this book, open minds need not fear innovation.

The rise of cryptocurrencies began with the emergence of Bitcoin. It is generally regarded as a counter reaction to our current financial system. Chapters 1 and 2 consider its launch by the anonymous Satoshi Nakamoto, as well as its functioning and essence as digital cash. Chapters 3 to 8 deal with basic monetary and financial theoretical considerations and place Bitcoin in the contexts of money, gold, central banks, the financial system, debt and volatility.

After monetary considerations, chapters 9 and 10 discuss technical and philosophical aspects of blockchain technology as well as license-free innovation that enables open-source software. Chapter 11 discusses Facebook's "cryptocurrency" Libra and how the project could be more beneficial to the US government as generally believed. Chapter 12 deals with the different cryptoassets and Switzerland, which has made a name for itself worldwide as the crypto nation par excellence.

Chapter 13 explores the rise of Ethereum, the second-largest public blockchain network after Bitcoin. This world computer relentlessly reveals the birth defects of the internet, as the reader will learn in chapter 14. Possible solutions are then discussed in chapter 15, which deals primarily with smart contracts that create a legal system for cyberspace. Chapter 16 sheds light on the new world of decentralized finance and how money protocols could revolutionize and democratize the world of investing.

Chapter 17 investigates blockchains that are not really blockchains: Tangle and Hashgraph. They shine a new light on Bitcoin and Ethereum. Chapters 18 to 21 deal with scaling endeavors for these two crypto networks, and the fundamentally different visions behind the two largest crypto networks become clear.

Chapter 22 is dedicated to the emotional topic of Bitcoin's energy consumption, looking at electricity costs and climate change. Chapter 23 then goes on to the legal system: What effects does blockchain technology have on our current laws? And chapter 24 finally discusses how non-central networks can be governed at all. Surely, the topic of tokenization should not be missing from a book about cryptoassets. Chapter 25 shows the advantages, but also the pitfalls, of tokenization. Chapters 26 and 27 return to the "big picture" once again. Blockchains allow us to completely rethink trust. What effects does this have on companies, authorities and states? Some of the prospects discussed prove to be quite inconvenient.

Finally, the last two chapters, 28 and 29, deal with the important aspects of privacy in the digital age. Will online identities one day be built on the blockchain? Are we moving into a global techno-panopticon, or does the digital space offer us a last refuge for privacy?

So, on the one hand it's about the here and now, but on the other hand it's about the future. Of course, forecasts and prognoses are a thing of impossibility. But even by naming patterns that can bring about long-term upheaval and change, much has been done. Therefore, the best forecast for the future is ultimately a precise description of current phenomena that have not yet made it into the focus of the general public.

THE MAIN CHARACTERS
NAME: KALI
PROFESSION: JOURNALIST
CHARACTERISTICS: ACCURATE, OBJECTIVE, CURIOUS
NAME: JAY
PROFESSION: CODER
CHARACTERISTICS: CLEVER, UPBEAT, WORKS EXTREMELY FAST
NAME: LORD IB VON KRATZ
PROFESSION: CHAIRMAN OF WCFG (WORLD CENTRALIZED FINANCIAL GROUP)
CHARACTERISTICS: HOT-TEMPERED, PARANOID, CONTROL OBSESSIVE
NAME: EVA
PROFESSION: DIGITAL ORACLE
CHARACTERISTICS: WISE, PATIENT, FORESIGHTED, HUMANOID
NAME: HERBERT
PROFESSION: FINANCIAL EXPERT & ECONOMIST
CHARACTERISTICS: GREEDY, ARROGANT, THE RIGHT HAND OF LORD IB
NAME: THE BANKEY
PROFESSION: BANKER & INVESTOR
CHARACTERISTICS: PROGRESSIVE, OPEN-MINDED FOR INNOVATION, SMOKES TOO MUCH

THE EXPERTS

NICK SZABO
A UNIVERSAL SCHOLAR, CREATOR OF BITCOIN PREDECESSOR BITGOLD. IS FREQUENTLY HELD TO BE THE TRUE FIGURE BEHIND NAKAMOTO SATOSHI.

ANTHONY POMPLIANO
IS THE BIGGEST BITCOIN BULL ON THE PLANET. WITH HIS NATURAL PANACHE HE'S KNOWN TO INSPIRE THOUSANDS OF PEOPLE. OCCASIONALLY KNOWS TO DRAG BANKERS THROUGH THE COALS.

VITALIK BUTERIN
A COMPUTER GENIUS, SUPER BRAIN AND CREATOR OF ETHEREUM. LOVES TO WEAR ECCENTRIC T-SHRITS. TAUGHT HIMSELF TO SPEAK CHINESE AND LIVES ALL OVER THE WORLD.

ANDREAS M. ANTONOPOULOS
BITCOINS STRONGEST VOICE. CONVINCED THOUSANDS OF THE PRINCIPLES OF CRYPTO-CURRENCIES. BELIEVES IN OPEN SOURCE AND PERMISSION-FREE INNOVATION.

MARK ZUCKERBERG
FOUNDER OF FACEBOOK. ENDEAVORS TO CHANGE THE WORLD WITH HIS OWN CRYPTOCURRENCY LIBRA.

MELTEM DEMIRORS
ADVOCATOR OF BITCOIN AND CRYPTOCURRENCIES. IS A FREQUENT GUEST ON TRADITIONAL MEDIA PLATFORMS AND WELL KNOWN FOR HER OUTSPOKENNESS!

CHRISTIAN DECKER
ONE OF THE BRAINS BEHIND LIGHTNING NETWORK. HE WORKS FOR A COMPANY THAT PROMOTES BITCOIN AND IS HIGHLY CONVINCING WITH HIS COMPETENT BACKGROUND.

NIKLAS NIKOLAJSEN
KNOWN AS THE FINANCIAL PIRATE AND FOUNDER OF ONE OF THE OLDEST CRYPTO FIRMS. A VERY LIBERTARIAN PERSONALITY AND WITH HIS RIGHTEOUS BEARING, ALWAYS ONE TO FIGHT INJUSTICE.

ELIZABETH STARK
IS A BIG FAN OF THE INTERNET AND LOVES OPEN SOURCE PROJECTS. ACTIVELY PROMOTES LIGHTNING NETWORK INTO POPULAR CONSCIOUSNESS AND IS CHARACTERIZED AS BITCOINS WARRIOR QUEEN!

CAITLIN LONG

A WALL STREET VETERAN WHO OVERTLY PROCLAIMED HER OPENNESS TO BITCOIN. IS CONVICED THAT WALL STREET WILL NOT VOLUNTARILY GIVE UP ITS HEGEMONY.

SATOSHI NAKAMOTO

THE MYSTERIOUS CREATOR OF BITCOIN. THE PERSON BEHIND SATOSHI HAS NEVER BEEN TRULY REVEALED.

JIMMY SONG

A CANNY DEVELOPER AND EDUCATOR OF BITCOIN CODERS. BELIEVES BLOCKCHAIN IS SNAKE OIL AND BITCOIN TO BE THE ONLY TRUE CRYPTOCURRENCY.

SAIFEDEAN AMMOUS

ECONOMIST WHO TEACHES THE AUSTRIAN SCHOOL. A BITCOIN AUTHOR AND UNRELENTING BITCOIN MAXIMALIST.

TUUR DEMEESTER

EARLY BITCOIN INVESTOR AND EXPERT ON THE BITCOIN MARKET. IS CONVINCED THAT BITCOIN IS THE FOUNDATION OF A NEW FINANCIAL SYSTEM. HE'S AN OPEN CRITIC OF ETHEREUM.

FABIAN SCHÄR

WORLDS FIRST BLOCKCHAIN PROFESSOR AT THE UNIVERSITY OF BASEL. IN ADDITION TO HIS ACADEMIC POSITION HE RESEARCHES POSSIBLE APPLICATIONS OF BLOCKCHAIN TECHNOLOGY.

ERIK VOORHEES

CONSIDERS HIMSELF A LIBERTARIAN FIGHTER OF FREEDOM. NEVERTHELESS, HIS WEAPON IS NOT THE SWORD, BUT RATHER A PATH OF DISCRUPTIVE REVOLUTION THROUGH BITCOIN. INTERESTINGLY, WITH HIS DIFFERENTIATED WIT IS KNOWN TO POSITION HIMSELF AGAINST BITCOIN MAXIMALISTS.

JACK DORSEY

CEO OF TWITTER AND ENTREPRENEUR. AS AN INVESTOR HE RECOGNIZED VERY EARLY THE POTENTIAL OF BITCOIN. AS A BITCOIN ENTHUSIAST HE DEVELOPS HIS OWN CRYPTO PROJECTS.

DIDI TAIHUTTU
THE BITCOIN FAMILY

ENTREPRENEUR AND BITCOIN ENTHUSIAST. HE SOLD ALL HIS BELONGINGS ONLY TO INVEST ALL THE PROCEEDS IN BITCOIN. HE NOW TRAVELS THE EARTH WITH HIS WHOLE FAMILY, DONATES CRYPTO AND GIVES SEMINARS ON THE FUNDAMENTALS OF BITCOIN.

THE RELIC OF THE ORACLE
HEY, YOU THERE! COME OVER HERE.
WHY ARE YOU HERE?
...THAT'S NONE OF YOUR BUSINESS!
TRY ME.
I WROTE A DEVASTATING ARTICLE ON THE CENTRALIZED FINANCE SYSTEM AND...
DENOUNCED THEIR DISTORTING EFFECTS!
GO ON! WHAT DID YOU WRITE ABOUT EXACTLY?
THAT WE NEED INDEPENDENT MONEY
...ABOUT THE DOUBLE-SPENDING PROBLEM.
IN ESSENCE, THE PROBLEM OF THE BYZANTINE GENERALS.
IT IS NOT SOLVABLE!
THAT'S FALSE! IT'S SOLVABLE!
SURE?! WHAT DO YOU MEAN?
TAKE THIS HERE! IT WILL TAKE YOU TO THE WHITEPAPER.
HURRY UP JOURNALIST! WE'RE LETTING YOU OUT!
WHERE TO? WHO ARE YOU?
SATOSHI!

Bitcoin gives you self-sovereignty.
Nothing else digital has that property.

Jimmy Song, Bitcoin Developer

1. Bitcoin and Its Beginnings

Economists, politicians and business leaders like to compare the hype around Bitcoin with the Dutch tulip bubble. Why do smart people use questionable comparisons to discredit Bitcoin?

The cryptocurrency is a thorn in the side of the self-proclaimed guardians of economic thinking, as it contradicts current economic theory, daily politics and economic behavior. They all too readily accuse it of being used by speculators, tax evaders and criminals of all kinds. But most important, many of them overlook the fact that Bitcoin is not just another digital currency but a cryptocurrency—an essential distinction.

Since Bitcoin enables the exchange of value over the internet, it appears to be a very common digital currency at first glance. A closer look, however, reveals that it has many things in common with cash. A Bitcoin transaction is therefore fundamentally different from an ordinary digital money transfer.

Today's economies operate almost exclusively with electronic money, whether it's U.S. dollars, euros or Swiss francs. Most consumers, at least in Western industrialized countries, also pay for goods and services digitally, whether by giro, credit card, online bank transfer or Apple Pay, PayPal or Revolut. Admittedly, these financial transactions are highly efficient and convenient.

But there is one crucial thing to keep in mind: every payment made in this way is recorded in a central accounting register controlled by a third party. This so-called intermediary monitors all financial activity and can theoretically censor or decline transactions that it does not agree with, or even confiscate funds (more on this in chapter 2).

Thus privacy remains only for transactions that are executed in cash. But there are ever more signs that cash, which is generally considered obsolete, will be abolished in the foreseeable future. It would then be almost impossible to pay anyone without this transaction being recorded in a centralized ledger. Financial privacy would finally become a thing of the past: in a world of digital currencies, control and surveillance are omnipresent (more on this in chapter 28).

As a cryptocurrency with the characteristics of digital cash, Bitcoin offers a way out of the dilemma. It has succeeded in solving the ancient Byzantine Generals' Problem using technological means.

Always in Consensus

Imagine several armies planning a joint attack on an enemy position. How can the generals, who are many miles apart, ensure that they reach a complete consensus on strategy and tactics before embarking on the attack?

A joint attack could lead to the conquest of the besieged city. If the generals' attack is uncoordinated, they lose the battle. Before the siege, the generals agreed to attack at dawn. But how can a general be sure that his colleagues will cooperate and stick to the agreement? Radio devices or smartphones have not yet been invented, and ancient signals such as torches or burning arrows would only warn the enemy. And even using messengers does not help. No general can ever be sure that messages will arrive correctly or that the messenger is not a traitor who actually works for the enemy.

For centuries, there was no solution to the Byzantine Generals' Problem. Then Bitcoin came along. In order to understand how it works, it helps to imagine the troops as computers in a network and the generals as copies of a database. In this database, known as a ledger, cryptographic encryption is used to record transactions and their creation dates. This creates a complete transaction history.

This is identical on all computers connected to the network. This means that each computer has an exact copy of the database. If an entry is now changed, the change appears at the same time on every other computer in the network. Or, more technically, as soon as a change occurs on one ledger and does not contradict the mathematics behind the Bitcoin program code, all other ledgers are automatically updated in accordance. In this way, the entire network is always in sync.

So, Bitcoin is considered to be the world's first non-central database in which there exists permanent consensus. Through Bitcoin's global network, people can exchange value today without knowing each other or needing a trusted intermediary—a controlling third party—to execute the transaction. The participants in the Bitcoin network can be sure that there will be no "double-spend" problem within the network (i.e., that no single bitcoin unit will be spent twice). The network detects and rejects deceiving transactions.

The non-central, cryptographically encrypted database distinguishes Bitcoin from any traditional digital currency and makes it what it is: the world's first cryptocurrency.

Bitcoin and other cryptoassets are stored in "wallets," and users can choose between two variants. A hot wallet is connected to the internet. In contrast, a cold wallet is completely disconnected from the web. A hardware wallet—for example, an external hardware device—is a form of "cold" storage, while mobile or web wallets without external hardware can be assigned to the "hot" crypto wallet category.

Important to know: The actual bitcoin are never located in the wallet itself; instead, they exist on the Bitcoin blockchain as booking entries in the shared general ledger, which is everywhere as well as nowhere. The wallets contain only the private keys that bitcoin owners use to access their systems. In contrast to a physical wallet containing cash, bitcoin are not lost if a wallet is broken or lost—provided that the private access keys have been safely written down somewhere else.

Clear Incentives

The story of Bitcoin begins on October 31, 2008. About a month and a half after the collapse of the U.S. investment bank Lehman Brothers and the onset of the global financial crisis, several cryptography experts on an obscure email list were contacted by a person called Satoshi Nakamoto.

"For some time now, I have been working on an electronic payment system that is completely peer-to-peer and does not require a trusted third party," wrote this unknown sender. His email contained a link to a document on a website registered two months earlier. The nine-page white paper described a payment system called Bitcoin.

It proposed the idea of a database spread over countless computers and updated every 10 minutes. But this was by no means new to the addressed cryptography fanatics and computer scientists. Even before the turn of the millennium, there had been similar approaches, but all of them had failed. The reason: none of the projects had been able to reliably solve the double-spend problem described above. So Bitcoin was met with rather little excitement at first.

But Nakamoto offered a solution to the double-spend problem. To solve it, he built a network of participants who each download a complete copy of a shared database. These participants are referred to as full nodes. Due to the open-source nature of the Bitcoin software, any person can connect to the system from any location, download the Bitcoin program code and become a full node. As decentralized accountants of the Bitcoin network, full nodes are aware of the current accounting status at all times and ensure that no payment is double-spent.

The system automatically compares each new transaction against a copy of the non-central database, which records all transactions ever executed in the Bitcoin system. The individual transactions are combined to form a block (for more information, see chapter 9). Each block consists of a unique hash, a kind of identification number that refers to the previous block. In this way, the individual blocks are interwoven chronologically to form a chain, the blockchain. They can be traced back to the genesis block (the very first block) and its original transactions.

This system creates a transparent transaction history that no one can change without the knowledge of the other full nodes. If a block undergoes a change—for example, if the content of a single transaction is subsequently adjusted—the identification number, or hash, of this block changes, which creates a discrepancy with the hash number of the next block. In this way, the system is protected from manipulation.

But how are new blocks added to the existing chain, and who ensures that they contain valid transactions? This is where the so-called Bitcoin miners come into play. Competitively striving to attach a new block to the blockchain, each miner tries to create a new block corresponding to the Bitcoin algorithm as quickly as possible using computing power. This is the case approximately every 10 minutes. The reward is new bitcoin.

If this sounds too technical for you, imagine this: the miner who rolls a six first for each digit on a 10-digit number will win the race. The miners control their results mutually and thus ensure that only valid blocks are integrated into the blockchain. Once a block is verified, the miners dedicate themselves to the next block and try their luck again (more about this in chapter 19). It is this ingenious incentive system that sets Bitcoin apart from its predecessors.

New Creation Myth

Today the Bitcoin ecosystem consists of several different groups. In addition to the miners already mentioned, there are developers (more on this in chapter 23), private end users and, of course, companies. All these groups often have different, sometimes even conflicting, interests. For example, users and businesses want low transaction fees, while the miners, who make money from them, advocate for higher fees.

Due to the different interests involved, it is difficult to implement changes within the system. Whenever a group wants to further develop the Bitcoin source code in one direction and this change does not appeal to other groups, the latter can threaten to "fork" the program code (more in chapter 10). This would result in a new Bitcoin variant and the network would be split.

Critics accuse Bitcoin of being "trustless." By this, they mean that there is no central authority behind the network that maintains trust in the overall system. However, this means that Bitcoin does not eliminate trust but minimizes it. Instead of an institution, it is based on mathematics and cryptography, which are ultimately backed by the laws of nature. Thus Bitcoin almost incidentally defuses an ancient trust problem that is inherent in all human relationships (more on this in chapter 26).

Since there is no central authority of trust within the Bitcoin network, the various actors—with their differing and often clashing desires and goals—try to keep each other in check. Because these participants somewhat influence one another without complete control, Bitcoin is often described as decentralized. However, the term is somewhat misleading since decentralization still requires a central authority. Since this simply does not exist in the case of Bitcoin, it is more accurate to refer to it as a non-central network.

This non-centricity, coupled with constant conflicts of interest, makes the Bitcoin system appear difficult to reform from an outside perspective. For many Bitcoin enthusiasts, however, this is a favorable feature rather than a bug, because non-centrality promises stability and resilience—not unlike the direct democracy practiced in Switzerland, for example. In both worlds, one waits in vain for an authority that speaks a word of power.

This applies even to Satoshi Nakamoto. The creator of Bitcoin has not spoken out in years. Nobody knows of the actual person or people behind the pseudonym. To conceal their true identity, Nakamoto has used at least three different email addresses, all of which were deliberately and carefully encrypted.

On December 12, 2010, Nakamoto sent his last message to the community he had been in contact with. Then he just stopped writing. And in April 2011, he even broke off contact with his core developers, who he had gathered around him like Jesus did his disciples. Just as mysteriously as he had appeared three years ago, Nakamoto vanished. As a godlike figure, he lives on in the minds of Bitcoin enthusiasts. And thanks to the blockchain, they can trace the path of the cryptocurrency back to its origin, the first block of Bitcoin, the legendary genesis block.

The parallels to the biblical story of creation cannot be overlooked. Just as mankind, after having been driven out of paradise, was supposed to cultivate the earth through laborious work, it is now the non-central community scattered all over the planet that must lead Bitcoin to success.

This creation myth is quite brilliant, ultimately reflecting Bitcoin's primary concern: non-centrality. The fact that even the founding force behind Bitcoin is unknown and has no central position of power underscores the integrity and value proposition of this idea. As well, it is extremely sophisticated—especially in the early days, the Bitcoin system could have been severely shaken or even destroyed through the manipulation or elimination of its founder. But without an identifiable face, such a thing was much more difficult.

ON TO THE GENERALS
BACK IN FREEDOM
ZZIIPP!
WHAT ON EARTH?! WHO ARE YOU?
HI KALI, I'M EVA. I CAN ANSWER ALL YOUR QUESTIONS.
WHAT ARE YOU? SOME SORT OF ORACLE?
COME WITH ME! I NEED TO SHOW YOU SOMETHING!
WHERE TO?
LOOK! THERE ARE THE BYZANTINE GENERALS.
SATOSHI SAID, THE PROBLEM HAS BEEN SOLVED!
THE MESSENGERS ARE NOT ALWAYS RELIABLE. AN ATTACK ON THE GENERALS CAN ALWAYS FAIL...
BUT THE BLOCKCHAIN ALLOWS FOR A CLEAR CONSENSUS! BITCOIN IS THE SOLUTION FOR THE DOUBLE-SPENDING PROBLEM!

The root problem with conventional currency is all the trust that's required to make it work. The central bank must be trusted not to debase the currency, but the history of fiat currencies is full of breaches of that trust. Banks must be trusted to hold our money and transfer it electronically, but they lend it out in waves of credit bubbles with barely a fraction in reserve.

Satoshi Nakamoto, Inventor of Bitcoin

2. An Evolutionary Counterrevolution

In his emails, the inventor of Bitcoin, Satoshi Nakamoto, repeatedly addressed a question that shapes the essence and philosophy behind the cryptocurrency: If money is king, who is king over money?

In the 18th and 19th centuries, a triumvirate emerged, one that has ever since managed our monetary system: governments, central banks and commercial banks. Commercial banks grant loans asked for by companies, private individuals and states, and as a consequence the money supply is expanded. Not only do central banks issue cash, but they are also responsible for keeping credit relations running. As the lender of last resort within this triumvirate, and endowed with the sole power over the base money supply consisting of cash and electronic central bank money, the world's central banks have to support the monetary system—which they did heavily after the outbreak of the financial crisis in 2008.

Over the last two centuries, this triumvirate has laid the foundation for a steadily expanding money supply and an impressive financialization of the world. It is to this triumvirate that we owe our current credit system and the modern equity and derivatives markets. Together with technological progress, the monetary system has led to unbelievable, unprecedented material prosperity.

But this development also has its downsides. Nakamoto rightly pointed out that central and commercial banks have repeatedly abused their power and the trust placed in them. As a prime example, he referred to the time before and during the 2008 financial crisis.

Today's money is a universal, abstract carrier of value. We not only use it to buy everyday necessities, but also to save up for an uncertain future. But what if money is suddenly no longer available or no longer worth anything? As shown by the rationing of cash withdrawals in Greece or the complete freezing of bank accounts in Cyprus in the wake of the financial crisis, such incidents can lead to feelings of insecurity, powerlessness—and anger.

Centralized financial structures can also be used to censor and silence critics. WikiLeaks, a platform dedicated to the disclosure of sensitive information about nation states and multinational companies, is one of the most controversial organizations around. Its supporters argue that it holds powerful institutions accountable by publishing anonymously leaked evidence of unethical behavior. Meanwhile, critics argue that WikiLeaks endangers national security and international relations and pursues a personal agenda against certain individuals or major powers.

Both views certainly contain kernels of truth. But instead of remaining neutral and staying out of the political and legal controversy, several major payment providers, including Visa, Mastercard, Bank of America, PayPal and Western Union, began rejecting donations to WikiLeaks in 2010—without any legal basis. For the nonprofit organization, which depends on donations, this was a hard blow. Even some critics of the platform had to admit that this was blatant censorship and a dangerous precedent. After all, there are countless other nonprofit organizations that are thorns in the sides of influential stakeholders.

But censorship is not the only way through which the triumvirate and its financial system exclude certain people. Worldwide, two billion adults are still considered "unbanked": they have neither a simple checking or savings account nor access to an electronic payment system such as Visa or Mastercard. Inclusion often fails because these people lack and cannot obtain verifiable identity. This is unlikely to change in the near future because traditional banks are not legally capable nor have incentives to provide everyone with banking services on a large scale.

Although Bitcoin will not lift these two billion people out of poverty overnight, the cryptocurrency is considered to be the most socially scalable network currently available. Long before Bitcoin was created, the Austrian economist, philosopher, anthropologist and historian Friedrich August von Hayek explained exactly what this means with reference to this quote from the English mathematician Alfred North Whitehead: "Civilization advances by extending the number of important operations which we can perform without thinking about them."

Hayek explained, "This is of profound significance in the social field. We make constant use of formulas, symbols, and rules whose meaning we do not understand and through the use of which we avail ourselves of the assistance of knowledge which individually we do not possess. We have developed these practices and institutions by building upon habits and institutions which have proved successful in their own sphere and which have in turn become the foundation of the civilization we have built up."

What Hayek meant by this is that humans are limited in their cognitive abilities, which prevents them from ever expanding their personal store of knowledge and interactions with other humans at will. But due to their inventiveness, humans are able to overcome their cognitive limits by developing institutions of all kinds (more on this in chapter 26).

Social Scalability

Language and writing are among the "technologies" that have most dramatically increased our social scalability. As Hayek rightly pointed out, we internalize these technologies until we can unconsciously use them to our advantage. Humanity has always discovered and made use of new technologies to increase social scalability. This includes the once revolutionary principle of double-entry bookkeeping, on which today's economic system is based.

About 500 years ago, double-entry accounting was widely used for the first time in emerging Renaissance Italy. Before its invention, each transaction was documented and stored in a single copy, and thus loss, deletion or alteration of an entry was much easier. Double-entry accounting reduced the need for trust in the counterparty by providing both parties with identical documentation of a transaction. This suddenly reduced the scope for manipulation.

Fraud can virtually be ruled out through the use of non-central triple-entry accounting, which is the way Bitcoin works. As we saw in the first chapter, network participants check the correctness of all transactions carried out in the network. Triple-entry accounting is likely to give social scalability a considerable boost, as it reduces the necessary trust in involved third parties by a considerable amount. Meanwhile, the triad of government, central banks and commercial banks continues to rely on double-entry bookkeeping. No wonder, then, that it feels challenged by Bitcoin's evolutionary—as well as revolutionary—character. And there is something else that speaks for the cryptocurrency: Bitcoin was not launched by any single or central party; it rose outside the existing financial structures and gained its significance through the use, encouragement and appreciation of single individuals. As a result, today Bitcoin is already more successful than conventional money reforms such as sovereign money, which grew within the existing system and therefore cannot go beyond its limited social scalability.

A conventional bank account still seems indispensable at present to manage financial matters. With Bitcoin, this is likely to change in the near future. The cryptocurrency has come to make the financial system work for everyone.

THE FINANCIAL WORLD IN TURMOIL
IN THE MEANTIME AT THE WCFG HEADQUARTERS (WORLD CENTRALIZED FINANCIAL GROUP)...
WE'RE BEING ATTACKED!
THE CRYPTO WORLD WANTS TO DESTROY OUR BUSINESS!
...AND BRING OUR WHOLE FINANCIAL SYSTEM TO HEEL!
THEY'VE NO CHANCE! EVERY DEVELOPMENT NEEDS FINANCING. AND WE'LL PREVENT THIS AT ALL COSTS!
WE NEED TO APPLY ALL LEVERS! BITCOIN NEEDS TO BE STIFLED BEFORE IT GROWS!

Money was on short distance debt, long distance gold.

Nick Szabo, Inventor of Bitgold

3. Money or Gold?

Bitcoin has the potential to revolutionize our money and financial system today. This raises an important question, which we will discuss in detail on the following pages: What kind of asset is Bitcoin anyway?

Ludwig von Mises, probably the most astute monetary theorist of the 20th century, described money as a generally accepted medium of exchange. Whoever adheres to this definition would come to the conclusion that bitcoin cannot be money. Today, only national currencies are widely accepted: U.S. dollars, euros, yen, renminbi, Swiss francs and others.

However, a completely different picture emerges among die-hard Bitcoin enthusiasts. For years now, the cryptocurrency has been used in the community as a medium of exchange. Some people even receive part of their salaries in bitcoin, and quite a few rely on it as a long-term store of value. There is no doubt in the minds of the Bitcoin community: bitcoin is money. And if one follows von Mises, they would know that it is fiat money that technically imitates commodity money.

The historically most important commodity monies are gold and silver. Since this kind of money is naturally scarce, its marginal production costs rise faster than those of other goods. Compared to ordinary goods, scaling the production of commodity money is therefore much more difficult—and expensive.

In his work *The Denationalization of Money*, the Austrian economist Friedrich August von Hayek, who we met in the last chapter, pointed out that all things can have what he calls "moneyness." After all, money is not something carved in stone that is fixed once and for all. This does not mean, however, that money is arbitrary. In the real world, there are certain qualities that make a thing "money-like" in the eyes of many people.

Money should primarily have a value or a purchasing power, which should last for as long a period of time as possible. One of the most remarkable characteristics of commodity money is that its marginal utility decreases less in comparison to the marginal utility of non-monetary goods.

The following example illustrates this: I would like to have one loaf of bread given to me, and perhaps a second one as well, but I would hesitate with a third one. Every additional unit of bread is worth less to me because the marginal utility of each decreases. Since, under normal circumstances, I have no use for so much bread, I would probably refuse to take a fourth, fifth and sixth loaf—I would not be able to eat this much bread before it goes bad. And trying to exchange it for other goods would take up time as well.

Smartphones, on the other hand, have a longer shelf-life than bread. If offered, I would certainly accept more than three. But even this product is limited in its marketability—at some point I will have equipped all my friends, acquaintances and relatives with smartphones—which is why the marginal utility of every additional smartphone would inevitably fall.

But this is hardly the case with monetary units. More money—at least from an economic point of view—is always good because it has the highest marketability, and this is virtually permanent. Due to its very slow decline in marginal utility, monetary goods are often hoarded, leading them to be high in stock. In economics, the level of stock (or the amount of a commodity) divided by its production over a specific period of time is called the stock-to-flow ratio.

Historically, precious metals have been among the most popular commodities to hoard. The stock-to-flow ratio of gold is currently around 64 years. This means that with today's mining capacity, it would take 64 years to produce as much gold as is currently stored. Bitcoin's current stock-to-flow ratio is approximately 25 years. However, this is likely to increase in the future as the production rate halves every four years.

There will never be more than 21 million bitcoin, all of which should be mined by 2140. Bitcoin's production rate is programmed to undergo a halving, which means that the number of newly created bitcoin units is cut in half, every four years. Today, miners "dig up" 12.5 bitcoin every 10 minutes. As of March 20, 2020, it will be 6.25 bitcoin, then 3.125 bitcoin in 2024 and so on. Therefore, like gold, bitcoin is a scarce resource. Currently, the number of new bitcoin is increasing by 3.8 percent a year, and this figure will drop to around 1.8 percent in 2020, so bitcoin's money supply will fall below the inflation target of central banks.

The production of new bitcoin requires electricity and thus incurs costs (more on this in chapter 21). In this way, bitcoin is similar to traditional commodity money: the more bitcoin a miner wants to mine, the higher the marginal costs of production. However, in the case of bitcoin, the program code will ensure that within the 10-minute period, only as much bitcoin can be mined as the code is currently programmed to release.

In 2024, bitcoin's stock-to-flow ratio will be around 119 years—twice that of gold. For some, this makes bitcoin the ultimate store of value. So, it should come as no surprise to anyone that bitcoin is often referred to as digital gold on steroids.

But unlike gold, bitcoin is limited to an absolute total, which is determined by the Bitcoin programming code. This makes bitcoin scarce in an absolute sense. In our "post-scarcity" world, where fewer and fewer things are actually scarce, a bitcoin will always remain one bitcoin. Although the supply of gold can currently only be expanded at high cost, there is still no discernible upper limit at this point in time.

One Last Way to Retreat

John Exter, the American economist and former vice president of the New York Federal Reserve, is famous for depicting the numerous assets of our financial system as an inverted pyramid. The wide range of financial derivatives, the riskiest securities, are at the top. They are followed by small business stocks, real estate, over-the-counter shares and corporate bonds. With each step down, the risk decreases.

At the lowest, narrowest levels are U.S. government bonds and cash, which are considered virtually risk-free. But if a disaster or total social collapse were to cause people to lose confidence in even U.S. government bonds and the U.S. dollar, they would almost certainly leave the pyramid and seek refuge in gold hoarded outside the financial pyramid—along with bitcoin, which theoretically is also located outside. Gold is traditionally considered to be at the very bottom of the inverted pyramid. But because gold and bitcoin have no counterparty risk—unlike every other security in the pyramid—modern depictions consider gold (and bitcoin) to reside outside of the pyramid.

The Hungarian economist Antal Fekete sees gold as the most important indicator of people's level of confidence in the financial world. In his view, there is no need for an act of trust or legal coercion to use gold in transactions. The same applies to bitcoin—to an even greater extent, one could argue. Like gold, bitcoin cannot be devalued overnight by any central bank and therefore has no direct counterparty risks. Those who store their gold coins at home under their mattresses, or their bitcoin in cold wallets—one of the safest storage options for bitcoin (more on this in chapter 1)—can always access the assets without having to rely on a third party. Meanwhile, government currencies are ultimately an obligation of central banks, and we can never be sure of their reliability since they are irredeemable today.

Due to these similarities, some market observers see bitcoin as a threat to the long-term position of gold as a store of value. They speculate that gold could lose much of its market capitalization to the cryptocurrency in the future. But gold is still very much in the lead: while bitcoin's market capitalization in mid-May 2019 was around $140 billion USD, gold stocks were worth over $7 trillion USD.

Speaking in favor of Bitcoin is the fact that our lives are becoming increasingly digital. Financial transactions, from simple online transfers to automated investment advice through robo-advisors, are almost completely digitalized.

Proponents of gold argue that the precious metal has seen many competitors come and go and that it has proven itself time and time again over a 5,000-year history as a store of value and a hedge against inflation. It owes this not in the least to its chemical property, which makes it almost indestructible. But the longer bitcoin lasts, the more the cryptocurrency will develop in a similar direction. This is demonstrated by the Lindy effect and the concept of antifragility.

Both concepts go back to the economist Nassim Nicholas Taleb. The Lindy effect states that the life expectancy of a nonperishable good increases proportionally to its age. So, the older something is, the more likely it is that it will continue to exist. The term *antifragility* means that a thing does not break but becomes more robust the more pressure it has to withstand, in accordance to the motto "What does not kill makes it stronger." So far, Bitcoin has been exceptionally antifragile, which in turn reinforces the Lindy effect.

According to current knowledge, Bitcoin is absolutely counterfeit-proof. Due to its cryptographic encryption, every bitcoin owner can publicly prove that only they own their corresponding bitcoin and that they are legitimate.

In addition, bitcoin is divisible down to its eighth decimal. The smallest possible bitcoin unit—0.00000001 bitcoin, or 100 millionth of a bitcoin—is called a satoshi and is named after the cryptocurrency's anonymous founder.

In other respects, bitcoin is already superior to gold. The portability of bitcoin is second to none. Bitcoin units worth several million U.S. dollars can easily be moved from one continent to another. This can be done either via the Bitcoin network or via a memorized private access key in the form of a 12-word passphrase—absolutely invisible to customs and other surveillance authorities.

In addition, Bitcoin is far less dependent on the internet than people assume. According to critics, Bitcoin would no longer be usable if there were a global meltdown of electricity and the internet. But it is foolish to believe that the Bitcoin community did not consider this eventuality as well. It is already possible today to transfer bitcoin via radio waves. At the same time, there are already satellites that can ensure the transmission of bitcoin. As with everything else, the leading cryptocurrency is taking giant steps forward when it comes to its own resilience.

Patience and Confidence in the Future

So far, we have seen gold and bitcoin as rivals that satisfy the same need for a long-term and non-corruptible store of value. But an alliance between the two investment forms is also conceivable. As financial analysts rightly point out, the cryptocurrency and the precious metal are currently negatively correlated. This means that if the price of gold falls, the value of bitcoin rises and vice versa. It can therefore make sense for an investor to include both investments in their portfolio instead of deciding between them.

At the moment, however, it is questionable whether this opposing trend will continue over time. With the increasing adoption of the crypto market, the correlation to other financial markets and asset classes is also likely to increase. Moreover, the objection that Bitcoin has so far only exists in a market environment characterized by high liquidity, low interest rates and weak volatility. Should central banks one day effectively reverse their expansionary monetary policy and let interest rates rise as a result, it will become clear whether the value of bitcoin will react differently or undergo a strong correction alongside other assets whose prices will fall.

Due to its high liquidity, bitcoin could be sold in the event of a downturn in the equity and bond markets, so that investors could better service their margin calls. This happened with gold at the outbreak of the financial crisis in 2008, when its price fell by more than 30 percent, despite record demand for coins and bars.

In a crisis, bitcoin would have the advantage of being held outside the financial system, so it could be disposed of at any time. If, for example, officials decided to use customer funds to rescue a bank by way of a creditor participation, technically called a bail-in, the power to access one's own money would be restricted all at once.

Not so with bitcoin. When the Cypriot government froze customer accounts for a month in March 2013, people began to buy bitcoin like crazy—based on its market capitalization of that time, of course (though at very low levels by today's standards). In a very short time, the trading volume increased considerably. During the crisis, the cryptocurrency proved to be a real alternative to a centralized national currency.

This is the case even if the value of bitcoin is subject to strong fluctuations. Supporters of bitcoin argue that the cryptocurrency is a cross-generational project, comparable to a large medieval cathedral whose completion has never been experienced by the people who have worked to build it their entire lives.

What all enthusiasts in human history have in common is a low time preference. The term comes from economics and expresses the willingness to put present needs aside in order to better satisfy future needs. A high time preference, on the other hand, describes people who would rather have something as quickly as possible, without really thinking about what it is they are getting.

A starving person, for example, has a high time preference: they want to get something to eat as quickly as possible, regardless of what it is. Meanwhile, a well-fed person has a low time preference: rather a good meal later than something hastily gobbled up now. The time preference varies from person to person and also changes from situation to situation.

If you buy bitcoin, you're better off with a low time preference. Anyone who constantly keeps track of the cryptocurrency's current price will not be able to sleep peacefully. It's patience and trust in the future that pays off.

THE FIRST CHAIN
AT JAY'S HOUSE
HEY KALI, HAVEN'T SEEN YOU FOR A WHILE. WHAT BRINGS YOU TO ME?
JAY, I'D LIKE TO INTRODUCE YOU TO SOMEONE – EVA!
WHAT ON EARTH...?
MANY HOURS LATER...
... AND THIS IS HOW THE BLOCKCHAIN WORKS!
WOW! IMPRESSIVE!
FULL OF ENTHUSIASM, JAY WORKS ON HIS OWN PROTOTYPE OF A BLOCKCHAIN.
ONE WEEK LATER
YES! IT REALLY WORKS!

The blockchain has given entrepreneurs much more options to enhance trades, transactions and add security to all members. A true innovation which will be in the benefit of all, the rich and as well the less fortunate ones by giving cost efficient solutions and creating global accessibility.

Michael A. Welti, Senior Banking Executive, Swiss Banking

4. To the Brave the World Belongs!

Even Bitcoin enthusiasts have to admit that this wondrous new type of asset seems paradoxical. In 2017 China tried to ban the cryptocurrency, the number of transactions pushed the technical infrastructure of the Bitcoin network to its limit, and buying and selling outlets for traditional investors were sparse. Nevertheless, the bitcoin price tripled within a few weeks toward the end of 2017 and finally reached its all-time high of over $20,000 USD per bitcoin.

Then in January 2018, prices fell steadily and heavily—despite the fact that the news from the crypto world was mostly positive and that technical development and integration into traditional financial markets were progressing. Paul Donovan, former chief economist at UBS, Switzerland's biggest bank, used William Shakespeare's words to describe his thoughts on bitcoin's price drop: "I come to bury Bitcoin, not to praise it." He couldn't have delivered his message any more clearly.

But as is well-known, people and things that are said to be dead live longer. It is easy to explain why the high prices of 2017 saw a steep correction. As always with revolutionary technologies, expectations were far too high at the outset, while the long-term potential was clearly underestimated. Bitcoin may still be a young phenomenon, but its history already shows that it follows a fractal price pattern: at each previous halving, in which the production of new bitcoin was cut in half, the price of the cryptocurrency reached a new all-time high.

It seems quite possible that Bitcoin was intentionally programmed in such a way that with each halving a new hype is triggered, attracting and strengthening interest in Bitcoin. In addition, bear markets (times of falling or dwindling prices) have so far allowed the community to concentrate, without much distraction, on the technical and infrastructural development of the crypto world, and to lay out the foundation for potential new all-time highs.

Persistent Animosity

Bitcoin has provoked people to think of the world differently—rather than centrally. The essential idea it promotes is to minimize something that is necessary for every economic transaction: trust. It is this unorthodox concept that causes persistent hostility and doom-mongering. This is why other blockchain projects are consciously trying to soften Bitcoin's revolutionary attitude by making compromises with the "old" world.

As we saw in the first chapter, Bitcoin is based on mathematics and cryptography. In its first 10 years, the algorithm kept its logic and stringency despite numerous attacks. Where residual trust in people is necessary—such as in software and hardware development or in mining—game theory provides incentives for disciplined behavior. Those who hastily ignore or categorically dismiss the crypto phenomenon do so at their own loss.

After all, Bitcoin offers you the rare opportunity to be the sole master of your own finances, letting you own your own money: if you have the corresponding private keys, you can access your bitcoin at any time and without the consent of third parties. This is not the case with online banking: for example, maintenance work on the part of the bank can make your money unavailable for hours.

Once Bitcoin transactions have been processed, no one can reverse them. And those who hold their own bitcoin do not have to fear that their bitcoin will be lent out in the background by a third party, as is regularly the case with securities held in bank custody accounts (more on this in chapter 5). Moreover, there is no central bank that can manipulate the supply of bitcoin, inflate their volume or expropriate savers by pushing interest rates into the negative.

If the financial crisis of 2008 has made anything clear, it is that there is no absolute stability in today's financial world, not even in Europe, which is spoiled by prosperity. Countless commercial banks across the world had to be rescued by central banks. In return, the latter have inflated their balance sheets beyond all previously known limits, while the former still or now have a thin capital base. So, bitcoin is also a hedge against the expansionary monetary policy that central banks all over the world have practiced in recent years, an asymmetric bet against the existing financial system.

Experts estimate that the construction and expansion of the new, non-central world will take another 10 to 15 years. It should not be forgotten that Bitcoin is just a basic internet protocol (more on this in chapter 14), very much comparable to a global triple-entry accounting system. Many other innovations, offerings and new business models can be built upon it, some of which, such as the Lightning Network, are already in the process of carrying out fast, low-cost, credit-card-style Bitcoin transactions (more on this in chapter 19). Since Bitcoin is an internet protocol, an unlimited number of additional associated protocols can theoretically be conceived on top of it.

A Wonderful Stroke of Luck

Bitcoin stands for a completely new, non-central financial system. The long-term nature of the cryptocurrency has the potential to shift the monetary values of short-sighted, impatient people to become patient long-term thinkers. This is why more and more investors around the world are asking themselves whether they should dare dip their toes into Bitcoin by investing some of their money. Currently, private investors are the main investors, and apart from a few hedge funds, the majority of institutional investors have not yet jumped in.

Many Bitcoin enthusiasts consider this a wonderful stroke of luck, which speaks to bitcoin's low threshold. After all, private investors have discovered this investment prior to banks, asset managers and pension funds. From the sidelines, however, most institutional investors are very closely watching the developments around Bitcoin.

It seems surprising that institutional investors have not yet included crypto investments in their portfolios, especially against the backdrop of the global investment emergency that has everyone desperately looking for some positive returns. The expansionary monetary policy of the central banks has immensely inflated the prices of many assets and reduced their yields. The reason that the financial world is still avoiding bitcoin at the moment, despite longing for returns, is probably due to its high volatility.

Price fluctuations of up to 20 percent within just a few hours can still occur easily with bitcoin. When U.S. equities fell by only 5 percent on February 6, 2018, Wall Street almost panicked. Institutional investors, especially pension funds, simply cannot afford such price fluctuations. What if a pension fund needs liquid assets and has to sell its cryptoassets? On a good day it would make an astronomical profit, but on a bad day it would lose a lot of money that belongs thousands of pensioners.

With regard to volatility, the argument often heard is that prices will stabilize once the bitcoin market has grown up and offers sufficient market depth. For this to happen, however, bitcoin needs the liquidity of institutional investors, the very ones currently staying away from the high volatility—the cat seems to be biting its own tail.

In addition, just like gold and foreign currencies, bitcoin does not generate a passive income in the form of interest or dividends, unless you participate in bitcoin mining. This, however, is extremely important for institutional investors such as pension funds, investment funds and insurance companies in order to meet their payment obligations. Staking offers the possibility of achieving a passive income. Network participants who keep their cryptoassets in a smart contract (more on smart contracts in chapter 15) receive compensation for this. While some small cryptoassets offer this option, at the present time they are hardly relevant.

The unpredictability of the overall market is also a thorn in the side of institutional investors. Precisely because Bitcoin follows its own rules, it seems even less predictable than the traditional financial markets. In contrast to conventional assets, there has hardly been any agreement on uniform valuation principles for cryptoassets. Since Bitcoin and other crypto protocols do not generate continuous cash flows, traditional valuation models such as the discounted cash flow method are of little use. New valuation approaches are already being discussed.

From the point of view of an institutional investor, there many points that make bitcoin a rather poor investment choice. At the same time, though, when talking to representatives of pension funds, one often hears the argument that because of their business model, they are committed to long-term thinking—there is no room for short-term speculation. The point they are missing, which the attentive readers of this book might be able tell them: bitcoin is by no means a short-term object of speculation, but is seen by the community as a long-term promise for the future.

An initially manageable bitcoin investment would therefore be in line with the mandate of a pension fund. In the U.S., at the beginning of 2019, the first institutional investors have recognized this and made a name for themselves by investing a small portion of their capital, following the motto "The early bird catches the worm." As long as the majority of institutional investors continue to wait to invest in bitcoin, existing investors will benefit from the low or even negative correlation their investments have with traditional asset classes. This in turn makes bitcoin a very reasonable add-on to their portfolios.

THE INVESTOR MEETING
WE'LL NEED SOME FINANCING FOR OUR BLOCKCHAIN.
HMMM...I THINK I HAVE SOMEONE IN MIND!
THE BANK
I HEARD ABOUT YOUR INTERESTING PROJECT...
THIS BLOCKCHAIN CREATES "COINS", SO MONEY?
EXACTLY! AND FOR THIS WE'LL NEED LOTS OF COMPUTATIONAL POWER. LOADS OF IT!
WHOEVER PROVIDES THIS TO US WILL BE REWARDED WITH COINS. ALL OF THIS IS DECENTRALIZED, NO INTERMEDIARY!
SOUNDS VOLATILE! COULD BE INTERESTING FOR VENTURE CAPITALISTS!
WELL, A STABLECOIN CAN HELP. IT'S LINKED TO REAL ASSETS.
I'LL SEE WHAT I CAN DO!

The securities industry's layers of ledgers are inherently inaccurate—they're never fully in sync, and therefore no one really knows who owns what. Bitcoin and blockchain will clean up capital markets.

Caitlin Long, Wall-Street-Veteran

5. Welcome to the World of Finance

Even though only a few institutional investors are currently invested in bitcoin, the leading cryptocurrency is slowly but surely arriving in the world of established finance. In December 2017, just as bitcoin set its preliminary price record of over $20,000 USD, two American stock exchanges, the Chicago Board Options Exchange (CBOE) and the Chicago Mercantile Exchange (CME), launched their trading of bitcoin futures.

A future is an exchange-traded standardized contract—a legal agreement to buy or sell an asset at a specified price at a set future date. For example, on the first day of a month, the parties involved agree on a future purchase price of around $9,000 USD and a deadline of the last day of the month, at which time the transaction—the purchase of one bitcoin—will be executed. On settlement day, they settle the difference between the agreed purchase price and the current market price.

This takes place in the form of a cash settlement in U.S. dollars. If, for example, the market price of one bitcoin is $10,000 USD on settlement day, the seller must pay the buyer the difference of $1,000 USD. If, on the other hand, the market price is only $8,000, the buyer owes the seller $1,000. The alternative is to physically deliver the agreed-upon asset, in our case one bitcoin for the price of $9,000.

The owners of such futures contracts can have exposure to the bitcoin price without having to hold bitcoin themselves. In this way, it's possible for someone to avoid having to store actual cryptoassets while being able to bet on rising or falling prices.

However, bitcoin futures contracts are not just "speculative." The original idea was to offer a financial instrument for hedging, in this case bitcoin holdings in a portfolio. Specialized bitcoin exchanges, in particular, such as Coinbase, Binance or Bitstamp are likely to benefit from bitcoin futures. The rationale behind this can be described as follows:

Whoever believes that bitcoin will rise in price enters into a so-called long position (i.e., buys bitcoin forward). On the other hand, if you expect a price correction, you go short (i.e., sell bitcoin on a forward basis). Depending on where the trading exchanges expect to see the bitcoin price land in the future, they build up either long or short positions in order to hedge their bitcoin holdings in the best possible way. Bitcoin mining companies are doing the same.

A Disservice?

The launch of the first bitcoin derivatives at the end of 2017 provoked the wildest speculations about the future price development: Would bitcoin's price go through the roof even more, as futures allow an even wider audience to participate in the mother of all cryptocurrencies? Or would the many critics of Bitcoin follow through on their words and bet on a price collapse? Might central banks even force Bitcoin to its knees with the help of futures and financial intermediaries?

A year later, it became apparent that with the launch of futures, bitcoin and the entire crypto world would actually slip into a bear market. Some Bitcoin sympathizers attributed the massive drop in prices in the first half of 2018 to price manipulation by futures traders. This held true in their view because banks and other financial institutions finally had the opportunity to push down the bitcoin price and must have done so. For hardcore Bitcoin enthusiasts, one thing was obvious: in the long run, traditional futures would most likely do the crypto market a disservice.

But there is a historical parallel that gives hope: When the first gold futures were launched on the New York Commodities Exchange (COMEX) on December 31, 1974, the price of the precious metal was also at an all-time high. Over the next two years, the price fell by almost half. But soon again in 1977, the gold price reached its former all-time high. From there, its value rose considerably.

Among Bitcoiners, there are also those who do not want to overemphasize the likelihood of possible price manipulations. And contrary to skeptics and neutral Bitcoin observers, the traditional financial world has many experts who see the launch of bitcoin futures at the end of 2017 as the first step toward greater mass adoption of Bitcoin and other cryptoassets. They see the decision of the Intercontinental Exchange (ICE) to create Bakkt as a trading platform for cryptoassets as an even bigger step. Intercontinental Exchange is an American company that owns exchanges for financial and commodity markets, and operates 12 regulated exchanges and marketplaces around the world—so it is quite a big player. In contrast to the bitcoin futures launched by CBOE and CME, futures contracts on the Bakkt platform will be settled in bitcoin itself. This means that bitcoin must actually be bought and held in safe custody.

With the introduction of such "physically" settled bitcoin futures, the launch of the first official bitcoin exchange-traded fund (ETF) also seems to be a little closer. Although previous proposals for an ETF have been rejected by the U.S. Securities and Exchange Commission, the regulator will not be able to delay approval forever.

The various bitcoin futures, the Bakkt platform for cryptoassets and a possible future bitcoin ETF all show one thing very clearly: After some daring hedge funds, private investors and venture capitalists, Wall Street is now beginning to turn to Bitcoin. This is often referred to as the "financialization" of the crypto world.

In simple words, the term means that more and more institutional investors, such as credit institutions, investment banks and fund companies, are intensifying trading and financial transactions with an asset—in our case bitcoin—and are launching or brokering financial derivatives such as futures or options based on it.

The immediate consequence of this financialization is the increasing liquidity of the underlying asset. Generally, this leads to more market liquidity, which in turn leads to more stable prices because volatility in the asset is reduced. It therefore becomes much easier, faster and cheaper to trade it, as more and more buyers and sellers enter the market. As we have seen in the previous chapter, more market liquidity and lower price fluctuations create the impetus for further institutional investors to enter the market.

The advancing financialization is therefore welcomed by pragmatic bitcoin traders—to the great annoyance of those Bitcoin users who fear that increasing market adoption by the established world will not benefit Bitcoin.

Unbacked Claims

Indeed, financialization also has its downsides. The pledging and short selling of assets, for instance, result in a greater amount of the underlying assets being traded than is physically available. For example, financial actors can legally deposit assets they receive as collateral for a loan, which can then be put up again as collateral for another loan. This is made possible by what are called omnibus accounts, in which securities are stored without being assigned to a specific owner. Re-pledging, called rehypothecation, leads to a long chain of repeatedly pledged assets, resulting in different parties having a valid claim to one and the same asset.

The economist Manmohan Singh has investigated such "collateral chains" for the re-pledging of U.S. government securities. For each government bond, there is a legitimate claim by three parties. If all parties were to assert their claims at the same time, two of the three parties would be left empty-handed because there are simply not enough U.S. government bonds available. Similar mechanisms led to the global financial crisis in 2008: when the music stopped, there were not enough chairs in the hall for everyone.

So while today's political thrust leans ever more greater towards individual transparency by establishing a global standard on the automatic exchange of financial account information (AEOI), on a systemic level, the traditional financial system is as fragile as Bitcoin is anti-fragile. Bloomberg opinion columnist Elaine Ou beautifully summarized the current affairs in this regard: "Financial institutions make people feel safe by hiding risk behind layers of complexity. Crypto brings risk front and center and brags about it on the internet."

Antithesis to the Blockchain

By their very nature, then, traditional financial markets create more claims to assets than there actually are assets. This makes today's financial system the antithesis of the Bitcoin blockchain, which is programmed so that there will never be more than 21 million bitcoin. The unfalsifiable, non-central database documents the ownership claims for each individual bitcoin or fractions thereof. In contrast to today's Wall Street, within Bitcoin's system there can never be more claims to bitcoin than there are actual bitcoin.

However, this can still be done off the Bitcoin blockchain, or "off-chain." Already today, exchanges and other financial institutions may trade so-called synthetic bitcoin. The more professional bitcoin and crypto trading on Wall Street becomes, the higher the risk that rehypothecation will be carried out on a large scale. So it may only be a matter of time before bitcoin is used as collateral on Wall Street and the extent of uncovered bitcoin claims goes through the roof. This would undermine bitcoin's algorithmically enforced absolute scarcity.

The same has already happened in the commodity markets, in which the amounts of paper gold and silver in circulation far exceed the actual physical reserves of the precious metals. These financial derivatives have a strong influence on the price formation of gold and silver, so in essence, the tail starts wagging the dog. This fate will not escape bitcoin either.

The only people who can mitigate this are the so-called hodlers, a force in the crypto world that should not be underestimated. This spelling mistake of the English word *holder* has established itself as a term to describe bitcoin holders with a long-term orientation. Most of them keep their bitcoin in "cold storage" hard wallets, one of the safest ways to store bitcoin. By keeping the private keys to their bitcoin with them rather than with a depository, the hodlers make it impossible for their bitcoin to be lent out or used as credit collateral without their consent.

The hodlers also have the option of initiating a fork, a splitting off from the Bitcoin blockchain by altering the existing programming code. The source code can be copied one-to-one or used as a template for a similar programming code (more on this in chapter 10). In theory, Bitcoin can be forked at any time—for example, if the Bitcoin community feels that Wall Street has created too many uncovered bitcoin claims via its financial derivatives, thus undermining the absolute scarcity of the cryptocurrency.

If the Bitcoin blockchain splits, you will at first have exactly the same number of bitcoin on both resulting chains. This is why forking is such a powerful weapon for the hodlers: they can move from one Bitcoin version to the next without losing their stocks. But this does not apply to unbacked claims on bitcoin. An unbacked bitcoin claim created off-chain and "out of nothing," so to speak, is not recorded in the distributed ledger and therefore does not exist on the Bitcoin blockchain. Nor does it embody a claim to bitcoin units in the new version.

For all those financial institutions that create unbacked bitcoin claims and use them as liabilities in their books, this is a real danger. Should the new version turn out to be the more valuable and decisive Bitcoin blockchain after a fork, the collateral issued by financial intermediaries based on the old version will, in extreme cases, no longer be worth anything. They would then have to make up for the losses, which can be rather expensive.

Will Bitcoin become an investment like any other, or will it succeed in doing what politics has failed to do in recent decades, making Wall Street safer and more transparent? Wall Streetization of Bitcoin or Hyperbitcoinization of Wall Street?—that is the question to be decided in the next few years.

GLOBAL, DECENTRALIZED!
IN JAY'S LABORATORY
HEY JAY, IS IT WORKING?
HMMM... I'M NOT REALLY SURE, KALI!
YOU BOTH NEED MORE INSIGHTS!
I CONNECT YOU WITH A KEY PERSON IN THIS FIELD!
FEW DAYS LATER
REALLY JIMMY? ONLY BITCOIN IS SENSIBLE? BUT WHY?
ONLY BITCOIN IS REALLY DECENTRALIZED! THE WHOLE THING MUST GO GLOBAL...
...CENSORSHIP RESISTENT...
AND PERMISSIONLESS!
WOW!!! AMAZING!
FINALLY!

As an experienced banker, my skepticism is natural. However, the longer I spend in this new decentralized world, the more likeable it seems to me. I am ever more convinced that in the banking world not one stone will be left standing.

The Bankey, Comic Figure

6. Declaring War on Wall-Street

The year 2018 would go down in Bitcoin's history as the year of the ICO, or initial coin offering, a new type of crowdfunding via the Internet. Investors invest bitcoin, ether or other cryptocurrencies in a promising project or business idea and receive the project's native cryptoasset or token in return (more on tokens in chapter 25). By issuing their own token, a group of people or company can quickly raise capital without having to rely on investment banks or venture capitalists.

ICOs mirror what is known in the traditional world of finance as initial public offerings (IPOs), which are held by companies when they go public. Thus it is quite tempting to regard an ICO as the digital counterpart to a classic IPO. This is not correct though. Anyone who buys a token through an ICO does not automatically acquire shares in the company. In addition, classic shares pay dividends and grant voting rights. While both are also conceivable with tokens, an investor cannot rely on any legal guarantees to enforce either of those in the case of an ICO investment.

Nevertheless, the American ICO market accounted for as much as 45 percent of the traditional IPO market in the second quarter of 2018. Compared to the venture capital market, its volume was 31 percent. This means that according to official figures, the total ICO volume was around $7.2 billion USD, while the U.S. IPO market had a turnover of $16 billion USD over the same period. The venture capital market's turnover was $23 billion USD.

But in the summer of 2018, ICO revenues began to dry up until September of the same year, when they came to a virtual standstill at just over $31 million in invested funds. The main reason for this decline were fixed costs and other expenses that needed to be paid by all the projects, which had collected cryptocurrencies during the hype. But now they had to liquidate the previously collected bitcoin and other cryptocurrencies. This led to downward pressure on prices, and the prices of various cryptoassets plummeted.

The numerous ICOs thus became a mortgage that would not be paid off for quite a while and which many people would lament over all the way into 2019. Yet, many people forgot an important fact while moaning: ICOs are proof that one does not need to go through the established players of the world of finance in order to raise a whole lot of money fast—and both efficiently and fully digitally.

An Act of Self-Liberation

During the ICO hype, investors not only lost a lot of money, but many of them also fell for fraudsters and charlatans. Of course, some of them were very careless and disregarded every obvious red flag. However, the fact that dubious ICOs were able to attract so many investors in such a short time frame is a clear indication of overregulated capital markets in the conventional world.

In fact, legal requirements make fundraising in traditional markets—even for over-the-counter investments—a very complex procedure. Anyone seeking capital must not only submit a promising business plan, which seems self-evident, but also comply with a number of publicity and accounting regulations. All these requirements make the world of investing a more and more exclusive event for major accredited investors.

This is one reason why the number of listed companies has been falling for years. Even up-and-coming startups go public later or don't go to Wall Street at all, because an IPO will cost them more than they'll probably earn. For example, an astonishing 29 banks were involved in the IPO of the American transportation service provider Uber, which goes to show that they all wanted a piece of the cake, driving up costs relentlessly.

The consulting firm Partners Group estimated in a 2018 study that the board of directors of a listed company wastes a quarter of its time on stock market bureaucracy today. It is therefore not surprising that Swiss entrepreneur Nick Hayek Jr. keeps publicly considering taking the Swatch Group, the largest watch company in the world, off the stock market—partly because of time-consuming accounting regulations. Although many of these measures are designed to protect investors and make markets more efficient, they all too often not only minimize an investor's risks but also their yields. As a consequence, ICOs have been hailed as an act of breaking free from the shackles of Wall Street to avoid the inflated transaction costs of the established world of finance. Money invested through an ICO is delivered directly to the startup; intermediaries such as stock exchanges, clearinghouses or notaries are not needed. In addition, tokens are traded without delay. Legitimate ICOs are therefore a gain for both capital seekers and risk-taking investors who want to support startups. And another plus of this revolutionary act of self-liberation: never before has a 16-year-old from Brazil, India or Mongolia been able to invest a few U.S. dollars in a future-oriented company based in Switzerland, Israel or Singapore.

As always, revolutions also lead to exaggerations and people pushing something of great use to exuberance and excess. But to ban ICOs completely, as China tried to do at the time, would be the wrong approach, as it doesn't make sense to ban the future and valid alternative.

So, while bitcoin offers a different option to money created by central and commercial banks, ICOs are an alternative to the centrally organized capital market. Investment banks have always acted as intermediaries between capital seekers and investors. Now there is a technical way to bypass these expensive financial go-betweens. ICOs are therefore considered a challenge to the traditional financial world.

Of course, established players are not going to give up their lucrative business without a fight. Most of them insist on replacing completely unregulated ICOs with regulated security token offerings (STOs). This is already happening—finally, some would add. Critics partly put the blame for 2017's ICO frenzy on regulators. Their argument: regulatory bodies failed their one and only task of protecting investors, because they did not bother to give token issuers a clear-cut security token standard.

The Swiss Financial Market Supervisory Authority (FINMA), Switzerland's regulator, put forward somewhat of an attempt by publishing ICO guidelines (more on this in chapter 12). Nevertheless, many token issuers around the world were very reluctant to relate their token in any way to a security because they feared that their corresponding regulator would take action against them. Ironically—as is with many other things—regulatory protection backfired on investors.

But better late than never, more and more regulators are now gradually warming up to officially embrace security tokens. Security token offerings are believed to be the next great thing, attracting large sums of money. So far, investments have come from primary dealers, but secondary markets are still rather nonexistent. The Principality of Liechtenstein has implemented the Blockchain Act to establish a legal basis for the token economy—a framework of new rules and changes to existing laws to allow for assets, rights and information to become tokenized. Meanwhile, other jurisdictions such as Switzerland, Singapore and Malta are betting on trusted exchanges.

AMONGST THE CONTROL FREAKS
WCFG
MY FRIENDS, WHO PRODUCES MONEY?
WE CONTROL THE MONETARY SYSTEM! WE PRINT MONEY AND DECIDE ON INFLATION - OR NOT!
THESE CRYPTOCURRENCIES WILL REVOLUTIONIZE WALL STREET
YOU BET!
ALL THESE CRYPTOCURRENCIES ARE DOWNRIGHT NONSENSE! OF COURSE WE WILL KEEP CONTROL!

You cannot isolate yourself from the consequences of others holding money harder than yours.

Saifedean Ammous, Bitcoin-Economist

7. Made and Designed for Central Banks

Libertarians predominantly hope that Bitcoin and other cryptocurrencies will one day replace government fiat money. And even if this takes a few years or decades, the crypto phenomenon has already proven that the state's monopoly over money is no longer absolute and is already faltering in some regions of the world. For example, in crisis-ridden Venezuela, where Bitcoin and other cryptocurrencies have been used as an alternative to the bolívar. Also, in Pakistan, Afghanistan and Zimbabwe, people have found Bitcoin out of necessity.

The cryptocurrency is following in the footsteps of gold: in the 19th century, the precious metal was the international reserve currency. During the First World War, many countries temporarily abandoned the gold standard to finance war efforts by printing more money. Following the hyperinflation in Germany at the beginning of the 1920s, and after the world economic crisis of 1929 and the catastrophe of the Second World War, the Allied Forces came to the conclusion that only a new world monetary system would guarantee global peace.

At the United Nations Monetary and Financial Conference held in 1944 in the small town of Bretton Woods in the U.S. state of New Hampshire, U.S. officials managed to conduct the negotiations in such a way that the U.S. dollar became the global anchor currency. While the U.S. dollar remained pegged to gold, the currencies of other countries became pegged to the greenback.

The government of the United States of America used this privilege to finance domestic and foreign investments after the Second World War. More and more U.S. foreign exchange reserves piled up in Western European countries as they increasingly generated surpluses in trading with the U.S. Under the leadership of French President Charles de Gaulle, more and more countries insisted on exchanging U.S. dollars for gold.

In August 1971, U.S. President Richard Nixon finally announced the suspension of the U.S. dollar–gold peg. So-called gold bugs (investors who are fond of the precious metal) regard this decision as a macroeconomic turning point in recent human history. As a matter of fact and to their point: since the world lifted its gold anchor, economic swings in the global economy have intensified. In addition, the global financial weight has shifted in favor of the U.S. At the end of the 19th century, U.S. equities accounted for 15 percent of global stock market capitalization; today this number is over 53 percent.

Thanks to its global currency, which is now uncoupled from gold, the U.S. can not only manipulate the financial markets and thus the global financial system at will, but it has also massively expanded its debt, which ultimately led to the 2008 financial crisis. In order to break the privilege held by the United States, countries around the world are pushing ahead with de-dollarization. For example, oil futures contracts denominated in the Chinese currency, renminbi, have recently been traded for the first time—up to this point, oil has only been paid for in U.S. dollars. At the same time, China is building a "New Silk Road," investing in Asia, Europe and Africa.

In addition to China, Russia in particular has recently bought more gold in order to reduce its share of U.S. government securities. The two countries have concluded bilateral agreements under which they intend to trade in the renminbi and the ruble instead of the U.S. dollar. But the European Union is not standing idly by either: rumor has it that the Europeans are working on a European payment system so that the Union can one day offer an alternative to the U.S.-dominated Swift system.

All in all, these undertakings are destabilizing the supremacy of the U.S. dollar. But what currency could replace it? Neither the euro nor the renminbi seems suitable. Therefore, some economists propose bringing into play a global world currency that is not issued by a single country. This would create no additional transaction costs in international trade, and no single party would benefit from being able to export its currency and exchange paper for real goods and services.

The director of the International Monetary Fund (IMF), Christine Lagarde, has already indicated that she wants to issue a cryptographically encrypted digital world currency. However, it would hardly deserve the name "cryptocurrency" since it would almost certainly be a centrally managed digital currency (more on the important difference between crypto and digital currencies in chapter 1). A genuine cryptocurrency truly contradicts the nature of the IMF; as an independent asset, it is not susceptible to political lobbying and manipulation.

Like Bitcoin. Since it has no counterparty risk nor is issued by a state and its central bank, which means that it is not administered and controlled by a single authority, it can be considered "neutral." Compared to gold, Bitcoin also has the huge advantage that transactions of any amount can be fully settled across all borders in just a few minutes. For international clearinghouses, such as central banks, this is actually an interesting, not to say lucrative, matter.

Geopolitical Power Struggles

Global trade would inevitably be facilitated by a single settlement currency. Nowadays, trade is conducted only indirectly: anyone wishing to buy goods abroad usually has to first purchase a foreign currency. This results in transaction costs that feed a huge foreign exchange market and keep it alive—a market that does not create any real economic value, if you will. Therefore, a global currency would lead most definitely to efficiency gains.

It seems unlikely that Bitcoin will rise to the rank of the official world currency. However, the community hopes that Bitcoin, as a laughing third, will benefit from the current geopolitical shifts. With the advancing de-dollarization, a transition from a unipolar, U.S.-dominated world to a multipolar world order is already happening.

China naturally has an interest in establishing the renminbi as the new global reserve currency. This is why the emerging country is taking action not only against the U.S. dollar, but also against Bitcoin. The Chinese government's attitude toward the cryptocurrency is ambivalent. Beijing has already tried several times to make life difficult for Bitcoin with bans and hard regulation—only to row back again and take another step toward the crypto world.

For example, China issued a ban on initial coin offerings in 2017 (more in chapter 6). However, this ban had to be relaxed when it became evident that ICOs continued to run underground and that the state was embarrassing itself by its lack of assertiveness. Moreover, it also lost income in this way.

For other observers, Bitcoin already seems to have achieved geopolitical relevance. The Commodity Futures Trading Commission (CFTC), a U.S. regulatory authority known for its caution and hesitation, approved bitcoin futures in December 2017 just one week after Russia, China, India and Brazil set up a new gold trading platform that bypassed the U.S. Coincidence? At the same time, the U.S. has the most to lose as the world becomes more Bitcoinized.

On the other hand, there is less at stake for Japan, the third-largest industrial nation, which has always been open to Bitcoin. In March 2017, the Land of the Rising Sun introduced the so-called Virtual Currency Act. Although this regulation does not clearly declare bitcoin a legal tender, it categorizes cryptocurrencies as a possible payment method. This is no coincidence: bitcoin trading volume is still highest in Japan compared to the rest of the world.

The most important reason for Japan's positive focus on the cryptocurrency might be deflation. Japan has been fighting against deflationary pressures for years. The national debt-to-GDP ratio of 235 percent is exorbitantly high. So far, Japan seems to have been able to escape the deflation trap more or less unscathed. But the country owes its own economic "upswing" above all to its central bank, which now not only owns more than 50 percent of all Japanese government bonds, but is also invested in over 77 percent of all Japanese ETFs. This makes the Bank of Japan a top 10 shareholder in 50 percent of all Japanese publicly listed companies.

Japan's officials are probably also aware that this development cannot be sustainable. Their open-mindedness toward Bitcoin can be seen as a possible indication that they expect traditional financial structures to die out soon and are therefore already experimenting with potential new ways today.

Central Bank Digital Currency

Should Bitcoin one day be politically recognized and have proven itself financially valuable for a longer period of time, it could then also become lucrative for central banks. Today, central banks around the world hold physical gold that serves as a safety buffer. Due to its non-centrality and uncontrollability, Bitcoin could be a welcome addition. Because of its digital nature, the cryptocurrency is also suitable for international clearing. In contrast to gold, which can only ever be transported under the highest security precautions, bitcoin amounts can be fully settled in just a few minutes.

In particular, Bitcoin could help central banks of smaller countries make their assets less dependent on large currencies such as the U.S. dollar or euro.

For the central bank of the small Caribbean island of Barbados, two economists have already explored this possibility in a working paper.

Bitcoin could also be of interest to central banks of those states that are commonly known in the West as "rogue states." Under the leadership of the USA, sanctions are repeatedly imposed against them. At the end of 2018, it became known that Iran was to be excluded from the international payment system Swift, which would hit the country's financial sector hard. It is very likely that such countries will in future rely on a neutral, global and censorship-resistant payment network such as Bitcoin—whether we like it or not.

Another scenario for the future is that bitcoin could one day be used by central banks as an asset item to hedge an e-currency issued by them, a Central Bank Digital Currency or CBDC for short. Some central banks are already further ahead than others. For example, the Swedish Riksbank is looking for ways to create an e-currency, and the People's Bank of China is also flirting with such an undertaking.

Central banks hope that a specially issued e-currency will give them more control over the money creation process. In Switzerland, for example, central bank money accounts for only about 10 percent of the money in circulation—the remaining 90 percent is created by domestic banks and lenders in the form of credit and demand deposits. These exist exclusively in electronic form—and interestingly, they are not legal tender but merely a generally accepted liability of banks. So today, when someone makes an electronic payment, they are paying with an implicit debt covered by the bank's asset balance, issued by a commercial bank. The central bank wants to weaken this quasi-monopoly of commercial banks.

The Swiss National Bank (SNB) is also rumored to be thinking about an e-franc. There are two ways in which a system with a digital currency issued by the National Bank could be designed. On the one hand, it would be conceivable for the SNB to offer a current account directly or indirectly via the commercial banks. The assets would be stored in a central database, and the e-franc would therefore be an entry in a centrally organized accounting register at the central bank itself. Each transaction would have to be verified by the central accounting system. Therefore, such an account-based architecture is also called "account-based."

Any private individual with an SNB current account would only appear to be the owner of e-francs, without actually possessing them. Since the National Bank stores all accounting entries in a central database, it would always have an overview of all transactions and could theoretically prevent transfers that could be detrimental to itself or the government. It could also introduce negative interest rates without any problems, especially if the implementation of e-francs goes hand in hand with the abolition of actual cash.

It would be a different matter if the e-franc were to be created as a digital token with the help of a blockchain or, more generally, distributed ledger technology (DLT). In this way, the e-franc would be called a "digital bearer instrument." In contrast to text, pieces of music or photos, which can be reproduced digitally at will, a digital bearer instrument is defined by the fact that it is the digital property of only one person (more on this in chapter 23).

In this way, the e-franc would exist as a digital possession that could be disposed of independently using the associated private access key. It would not be just an entry in the database of a third party. Private individuals could store their e-francs in a private, digital wallet. This is why this model is called "value-based."

The best-known and first digital bearer instrument is Bitcoin. Would an e-franc based on blockchain technology be the better version of Bitcoin because it is issued by the trusted central bank? By using DLT and decentralizing the network, the central bank would increase resilience. In a way, this variant of the e-franc would resemble today's cash system. As with cash, settlement would be direct and final, and payer and payee would not be directly dependent on a third party.

Whether anonymity would be given to the same extent does not seem clear at this stage. The data could be cryptographically encrypted. So-called "zero-knowledge proofs" (more on this in chapter 29) would nevertheless ensure that there is a consensus on the validity of a transaction within the e-franc's network. However, the additional encryption would increase the complexity and potentially make the system slower and less scalable.

That being said, the distinction we already made in chapter 1 continues to apply: Cryptocurrencies such as Bitcoin are beyond the control of any central authority, while a digital currency such as an e-franc issued by the Swiss National Bank can be controlled centrally, taxed more easily and, if necessary, manipulated (for example, be inflated). All participatory nodes in its blockchain network would be known to the National Bank to maintain control of the system. An absolute nightmare for any libertarian-minded person.

BATTLE OF THE GIANTS
THE GENESIS BLOCK WAS CREATED. JAY'S AND KALI'S OWN BLOCKCHAIN HELPED THEM TO BETTER UNDERSTAND BITCOIN. NOW, THEY WANT TO KNOW MORE!
I'LL CREATE A WORLD COMPUTER,
...A PROGRAMABLE BLOCKCHAIN FOR A DECENTRALIZED WORLD!
VITALIK, ETHER WILL NEVER BE ABLE TO COMPETE WITH BITCOIN! ETHEREUM IS NOT SCALABLE!
IT'S THE YAHOO OF THE CRYPTO WORLD!
TUUR, YOU'RE A BITCOIN MAXIMALIST!
NO, I'M A BITCOIN REALIST!
HMMM...BOTH HAVE THEIR PROS AND CONS! WHAT WOULD EVA SAY ABOUT THEM?

In addition to the Internet of Information, which is already available to all, public blockchains will create the Internet of Values. Control will be decentralized, asymmetries will be eliminated and Blockchain will change the way we act and interact with everything.

Bastiaan Don, CEO Token Factory Switzerland

8. From Bitcoin to Stablecoins

The biggest weakness of Bitcoin is still considered by most to be its persistent volatility. Without price stability, the cryptocurrency will never be able to gain a foothold in everyday life, but will remain a marginal phenomenon forever, according to the frequently heard opinion.

What many analysts fail to consider: the irrevocably disinflationary nature of Bitcoin—the upper limit for newly created units defined in the programming code—makes price fluctuations unavoidable. The rigid creation algorithm makes Bitcoin inflexible on the supply side. Supply cannot adapt quickly enough to fluctuating demand.

Hardcore Bitcoiners, on the other hand, see this inherently disinflationary character of Bitcoin as its greatest advantage. Because supply lags behind demand, the currency has a deflationary effect—the price of goods measured in bitcoin falls over time. This allows people to look to the future and increases savings.

Of course, this view immediately brings on the critics. They argue that Bitcoin can never be the basis of a functioning economy, since deflation always causes a downward spiral in prices, which ultimately forces the economy to its knees, resulting in the usual consequences, including unemployment in particular.

What is often overlooked when bringing forth this argument: saving never replaces consumption; it merely postpones part of it into the future. Other needs, above all the basic needs essential for survival, are satisfied immediately by people. In an economy that is not driven by the creation of new money, deflationary horror scenarios are unlikely to have the explosiveness attributed to them in today's economy. Deflation and its economic distortions are to be feared above all if they have been preceded by a previous expansion of the money supply—as is currently the case.

Critics accuse bitcoin traders of speculation, but even this is not bad in and of itself. On the contrary, there's the argument that more people should speculate on bitcoin! Speculation leads to more transactions and thus more market depth. Ongoing and increasing trade volume in turn leads to price fluctuations being smoothed out more quickly, as there is a larger pool of "speculators" and thus more liquidity.

Three Types of Stablecoins

Economists of the Austrian School consider price fluctuations to be a natural phenomenon. They consider price stability that mainstream economists strive for to be an illusion, since there can be no such thing as stable prices in a dynamic economy, according to their main argument.

Friedrich August von Hayek, their best-known representative, however, saw it somewhat differently: Confronted with inflation all his life, he longed for price-stable money, because only that would make long-term trust relationships, and therefore economic growth, possible. In addition, he argued, hardly anyone wanted to take on longer-term debts in a monetary unit that was subject to strong fluctuations in value. An unstable currency would also make it more difficult to maintain a company balance sheet with assets, wage payments and equity.

Most entrepreneurs would agree with Hayek. Volatile prices simply increase business risks and discourage making contracts that last over longer periods of time. In response—in order to meet the need for price stability—the crypto world has dared to create stable cryptocurrencies, so-called stablecoins.

In a short period of time, they have sprung up like mushrooms. While at the end of 2017 the number of these projects was relatively manageable at around 30, by the end of 2018 it rose to over 180. Currently, there are more than 220 stablecoins. It is hardly surprising that this crypto category experienced enormous growth with the advent of the bear market. But it remains to be seen whether the demand for stablecoins is actually as high as all the venture capitalists, who have launched most of the stablecoins, think. Similar to the thousands of ICO projects that first soared to lofty heights before crashing (more on this in chapter 6), consolidation is also likely to take place here in the future.

So far, three basic types of stablecoins can be distinguished. The most popular approach is that of a stablecoin backed by government fiat currencies. In addition, there are somewhat less conventional attempts to create stablecoins backed by other cryptoassets, or even unbacked (more on cryptoassets in chapter 12).

Backed by Money or Gold

The simplest variant of a stablecoin is linked, or pegged, to a national fiat currency—preferably the U.S. dollar. The issuance of such a cryptocurrency is accompanied by the promise that it is fully backed by U.S. dollars. The largest stablecoin, Tether, with a market capitalization of over $2 billion U.S. in May 2019, works according to this principle.

You might assume that stablecoins of this kind have an important flaw: they presuppose confidence in a centrally organized issuer—the very entity that cryptocurrencies are trying to make obsolete. Whoever holds Tether has to trust those responsible behind the project that they have the corresponding number of U.S. dollars for the Tether they issue.

For some time now, there has been a heated debate about whether all Tethers are really backed by sufficient reserves. There is no obligation to redeem Tether coins by exchanging them for the corresponding amount of U.S. dollars. In April 2019, the news reached the public that Tether is actually not backed 100 percent by reserves. Surprisingly, neither the bitcoin nor the Tether price really collapsed. This could be an indication that even the risk-averse investors of the crypto world give little thought to a full reserve.

The Swiss franc–backed CryptoFranc (XCHF) wants to do better. It was issued by Swiss Crypto Tokens, a subsidiary of Bitcoin Suisse, a pioneer in the field. The issuer is trying to defuse the obvious confidence problem in various ways. For example, the portfolio used as collateral does not include real estate or other assets but consists of physical banknotes that are held in safe custody. In addition, this cash is insured at its current market value. Every month, the relevant parameters are checked and published by an auditor.

Neither the Swiss franc nor the U.S. dollar, but gold is used to cover the cryptocurrency Digix DAO. This is an open-source project aimed at tokenizing valuable assets such as gold—and potentially other precious metals such as silver at a later date (more on tokenization in chapter 25). The DGX token created for this purpose is intended to grant the holder the right to one gram of gold, which is stored in a certified vault in Singapore. As a stablecoin, the DGX token is intended to imitate the stability of gold and other precious metals.

This concept bypasses government fiat currencies, but an important problem remains: the more widespread a stablecoin of this type becomes, the less efficient its "business model" becomes. A fractional reserve system, in which not all issued tokens are fully backed with physical gold or money, seems to be the inevitable fate of every stablecoin of this type.

Less Efficient Overcollateralization

In order to solve at least the problem of central control and administration, the innovative possibility of securing a stablecoin with one or more other cryptoassets is an option. MakerDAO has popularized this approach. Two different tokens are relevant for the project: Maker and Dai. Maker tokens embody voting rights. They are most similar to shares, but they do not pay dividends. If you want to have a say in the future of the MakerDAO system, you have to buy Maker tokens.

The Dai token is the actual stablecoin, the value of which should always correspond to one U.S. dollar. In order to maintain this parity, Dai is backed with the second-largest cryptoasset, ether. As the developers behind MakerDAO have already announced, users will be able to back the stablecoin using other cryptoassets as collateral in the future.

How can Dai be price-stable if ether used as backing has the typical volatility of a cryptocurrency? MakerDAO tries to solve this dilemma with overcollateralization: only half a Dai is issued per ether. Ether worth $2,000 USD thus back Dai worth $1,000 USD. If the price of ether falls by 25 percent, the originally issued stablecoins would be backed by an equivalent of $1,500 USD and can thus still be valued at the nominal value of one U.S. dollar.

But why would anyone want to enter into this capital-intensive and therefore inefficient scheme of overcollateralizing? Quite simply, it serves to leverage one's own crypto finances. With ether worth $2,000 USD, $1,000 USD can be created in Dai. If this $1,000 in Dai are used to buy another $1,000 in ether, the leverage effect will result in an ether position of $3,000, backed by only $2,000 in ether. If the ether value doubles, you will own $6,000 USD worth of ether instead of just $4,000.

But what if ether suffers a massive loss? In order to maintain Dai's U.S. dollar parity, the MakerDAO system would actually have to sell the ether held as collateral to support Dai. This would hurt the backing behind Dai even more; hence the high overcollateralization, which is supposed to make Dai crisis-resistant.

Central Bank, but Decentralized

The third type of stablecoin does not require any collateral at all. This idea can be traced back to Friedrich August von Hayek, who postulated similar things for paper currencies in his works.

Following the quantity theory of money, the price stability of this stablecoin is achieved by increasing or decreasing the money supply as needed. Algorithms take over the control of the amount of money or tokens allocated—in the case of government fiat currencies, to the central banks. The price of the stablecoin is kept as close as possible to the U.S. dollar or another national fiat currency via so-called smart contracts.

If the price of the stablecoin rises above the U.S. dollar mark due to a demand overhang, the algorithm lowers the price again by creating new stablecoins. If, on the other hand, there is too much supply floating around and the price is thus below one U.S. dollar, the situation becomes more difficult. The algorithm is required to buy back excess stablecoins. But what money does it use?

Most stablecoin projects have funds available from ICOs or private investment rounds. If these are used up, the issuance of bonds or so-called seigniorage shares is an option. These entitle the holder to buy and get stablecoins in the future.

Without a steady inflow of monetary resources, this system will collapse sooner or later. Even the promise of future seigniorage shares will only work if the stablecoin continues to grow—which brings it suspiciously close to pyramid schemes. Quite a few market observers therefore consider such unbacked stablecoins to be ticking time bombs.

The idea of non-centrally mimicking a central bank via smart contracts may be fascinating. However, unbacked algorithmic stablecoins are unlikely to be sustainable in the long run. Without the monopoly over money, it seems to be only a matter of time before the forces acting on a stablecoin tear it apart. But even the monopoly over money does not guarantee stability. Again and again in the history of currencies, central banks have failed to keep national fiat currencies stable. Particularly problematic were the times when officials simultaneously strived for a free movement of capital, an autonomous monetary policy and a fixed exchange rate.

This so-called trilemma of monetary policy cannot be resolved. The fact that stablecoins attempt to solve it in a non-central way does not make things any easier. Although the idea of a decentralized central bank is tempting, it is likely to remain a utopia for the time being. Unless, of course, projects such as MakerDAO succeed in the long term and thus prove the opposite. In the meantime, stablecoins backed by national currencies—although not quite so sexy from a true crypto perspective—have been able to develop a real use case for businesses around the world. Companies that are active on a global scale can use stablecoins to do business more effectively. Stablecoins can serve as a means to circumvent arbitrary capital controls as well as high remittance fees charged by banks and other players for international money transfer.

THE BITCOIN BLESSING
ARGHH! THE STOCK AND BOND MARKETS ARE CRASHING!
ANOTHER BLACK MONDAY!
SELL EVERYTHING!
I CAN'T RETRIEVE ANY MONEY!
MY BANK IS ALSO CLOSED!
I WANT MY MONEY!!!
THE WCFG HAS FROZEN OUR SAVINGS!
CHECK THIS OUT! MY FUNDS ARE ACCESSIBLE AT ANY TIME!
I HAVE BITCOINS - STORED IN MY HARD WALLET!
YES, I ALSO HAVE ONE - JUST GREAT!
THE VALUE OF BITCOIN IS RISING MASSIVELY! INCREDIBLE!!!
MY FIRST BITCOIN-BENTLEY!

While the number of applications blockchain can serve is massively overrated, its effect in those areas, in which the technology can be used successfully is massively underrated.

Fabian Schär, Professor at the University of Basel

9. From Bitcoin to Blockchain

Bitcoin has set itself the goal of shaking the overly powerful world of banking and finance, not by force or coercion, but by argument and conviction. A little over 500 years ago, Martin Luther nailed his 95 Theses to a church door; a decade ago, Satoshi Nakamoto uploaded his white paper to a website—both actions intended the same thing: to show the powerful that they had gone too far. Some banks have recognized the danger and are trying to stymie the ongoing Bitcoinization of the investment world by integrating the technology behind Bitcoin into their own systems. Specifically, what they are trying to co-opt is the blockchain mentioned in the first chapter.

It is in the nature of language and society that a trendy term gets used in an inflationary manner, thus losing all meaning over time. Whether in the cultivation and trade of environmentally friendly bananas, in reforestation or in finance—the blockchain is considered the solution to all earthly problems. Can a single technology really solve such a wide variety of problems? To see the possibilities, it is worth making a short detour to its origins.

The term *blockchain* is commonly attributed to Satoshi Nakamoto. Interestingly enough, the anonymous founder of Bitcoin never used the word himself, neither in the Bitcoin white paper nor anywhere else. Instead, he spoke of a "chain of hash-based proof-of-work," a "chain of blocks" and a "timechain," merely trying to find catchy words and images for the mathematical bits and bytes that ultimately underlie the technology. For Nakamoto, the concept of the blockchain was only part of a larger whole. The blockchain itself describes *only* the chronological linking and identification of data. Hence the term *timechain*.

The recorded data are property titles that are secured by digital signatures. The timechain links this data in such a way that a transaction history of ownership relationships is created, which provides information about who owns how much of what and when. In the case of Bitcoin: in accordance with Nakamoto's approach, data showing who owns how many bitcoin units and when is recorded in this so-called distributed ledger and is always publicly accessible (more on this in chapter 1).

The Bitcoin software is available for free on the internet. When you download the entire Bitcoin protocol onto your computer, you automatically download the entire transaction history, which updates every 10 minutes. Since a copy of the same ledger is installed on thousands of computers, or "nodes," the individual network participants ensure that no one can cheat on the system. To enable this distributed ledger to defy hacker attacks, Nakamoto integrated the so-called proof-of-work mechanism, which ensures that the continuation of and any changes to the blockchain require extremely high costs (more on this in chapter 21). It is not completely impossible to change the transaction history, but as the Bitcoin network becomes more widespread and capitalized, it becomes increasingly difficult to manipulate the network.

Bitcoin is an open-source project. This means that any person can propose changes to be implemented, if approved by the developer community. Because various Bitcoiners always keep an eye on the source code, quick or furtive fixes at the development level are virtually impossible (more on this in chapter 23).

The utility of and fascination with blockchain as a technology that revolutionizes all areas of life are fueled by the combination of the following five features: 1) the combination of data into a blockchain, 2) digital, unforgeable signatures, 3) the distribution of the ledger on numerous computers, 4) the proof-of-work mechanism to prevent network attacks 5) and the open-source character. These five elements make the blockchain a hacker-resistant, solid, transparent, non-central trust machine. However, at the same time, the combination of these characteristics also makes it resource-intensive, slow, poorly scalable and hardly legally regulable.

Private Blockchains

Under the motto "Blockchain without Bitcoin," centralized companies in traditional industries also praise the blockchain as the new IT and communications technology, and have begun to implement their first blockchain projects individually or in collaboration. However, die-hard Bitcoin proponents argue that using blockchain technology for established business purposes is completely uneconomical. The new technology is not a "cloud" for distributed data storage because it is extremely inefficient when used in a centralized system.

An old piece of advice sums up this opinion: "Cobbler, stick to your last." From a true Bitcoiner's point of view, a blockchain is only necessary and useful if you want to eliminate a bank, a large corporation or, more generally, a centralized controlling authority and establish non-centralized trust relationships.

So, are banks currently tossing a lot of money out the window with their well-meaning blockchain projects? In order to unravel the paradoxical situation, it helps to distinguish between different blockchain variants. In concrete terms, we are talking about public, private and federated blockchains.

But already, the argument starts all over again. Bitcoin supporters argue that this distinction makes no sense. In their opinion, private and consortium blockchains are simply not real blockchains. The clever minds behind "blockchain for business" projects bring forth the counterargument that public and private blockchains are two completely different entities that pursue completely different goals.

In their experience, private blockchains lead to immense efficiency gains. In everyday business, they argue, companies communicate continuously with each other. This happens on the one hand via fully digitized and automated interfaces, while other processes are still paper-based. On the other hand, each participant often maintains their own database. Keeping this database up-to-date and consistent at all times is difficult, prone to errors and incurs high costs.

From the point of view of their proponents, private or consortium blockchains create a so-called "single point of truth." In this way, all participants would always have up-to-date and consistent data at their disposal—there would be only one "truth" that all participants could see at any time. Such systems make the cumbersome manual exchange and comparison of data between companies and individual areas superfluous. In addition, they can also help large corporations to eliminate expensive intermediaries in areas such as payment transactions, asset management and logistics.

But for these purposes, Bitcoiners are quick to point out, decentralized databases would also be sufficient—a statement that is both right as well as wrong. In a private blockchain, a company operates the nodes itself (more on this in chapter 1), which together form the internal network. The corresponding blockchain and its underlying protocol are owned by the company, which has sole control over the private blockchain. This may be completely necessary in some situations—for example, if a company has to maintain confidentiality or access restrictions, but at the same time wants to be connected to a public blockchain and participate in its ecosystem. This is hardly possible with an ordinary database.

Federated Blockchains

In contrast to the private version, a federated blockchain is controlled by a group consisting of independent actors. As a kind of administration, it decides together who can join the network as a node and who can view the transaction history. Like an internal company blockchain, it is not free of permissions, and the number of nodes is chosen by the administration.

What a blockchain ought to be is not carved in stone. Thus, in all three versions, there are different manifestations of the basic principles, with the public blockchain forming one end of a continuum and the private blockchain the other. A blockchain that has all five of the characteristics described above can be described as open and permissionless. Every person in the world connected to the internet theoretically has access to an open and permissionless blockchain.

In contrast, some of those characteristics are not present in permissioned blockchains. This makes them more susceptible to manipulation. If only a few nodes record and validate information, then it is of course more vulnerable to failures, corruption and hacker attacks. It is therefore a good idea to put any blockchain rhetoric to the acid test. A blockchain that is not very transparent, requires authorization and is spread over a few nodes is a completely different matter than a public, permissionless blockchain whose network consists of thousands of independent nodes.

The fact that software giants like IBM and SAP sing their own praises about their blockchain solutions, or the soccer association UEFA wants to sell tickets via a blockchain, or banks swagger about their own blockchain-based projects may in many cases simply be the marketing efforts of companies that are jumping on the bandwagon of the blockchain hype. Marketing attracts new customers and can lead to technically outdated systems being subjected to long-overdue improvements—even if these have little to do with blockchains. Or to sum it up with Bonini's paradox, which the French poet

Paul Valéry summed up in a nutshell: "Everything simple is false. Everything complex is unusable."

Bitcoin is the first and still most relevant public blockchain. Due to the pioneering effect, the large developer community and the high business interest in Bitcoin, this is likely to remain the case. However, it is also plausible that other public blockchains—above all, Ethereum—will catch up (more on Ethereum in chapter 13).

Whether private and federated blockchains can survive in isolated form is more questionable. We know from the history of the internet that intranets (i.e., private networks) were particularly popular in the beginning. With increasing development, however, these were replaced by ever better and safer open internet solutions. Intranets have not disappeared, but they play only a subordinate role in a few large corporations. A similar fate is also likely to befall private and consortium blockchains, or they may just be turned into minor sidechains of public blockchains.

FREEDOM
IT'S JUST GREAT TO HAVE A FREE AND CARE FREE LIFE.
YES, THIS IS TRUE LUXURY! IT WAS THE RIGHT DECISION TO SELL EVERYTHING AND INVEST ALL IN BITCOIN!
A CALL FOR YOU!
JAY
OH, IT'S BEEN A LONG TIME!
HEY DIDI, THE BITCOIN PRICE IS CRAZY AND YOUR OLD HOUSE IS SELLING AT A BARGAIN!
DON'T YOU WANT TO COME BACK?
NO WAY, WE ARE LIVING OUR DREAM WITH BITCOIN! IT'S THE FUTURE!
DAD, LOOK! A PACIFIC BASTARD TORTOISE. THEY'RE JUST AS RARE AS BITCOIN!
I WONDER WHICH ARE RARER!

If you have a system where conditions are more open, free and efficient, there's no question about the outcome. The free open and efficient system beats the closed, centralized and inefficient system every time.

Andreas M. Antonopoulos, Bitcoin-Expert

10. To Fork or Not to Fork

In the traditional world of finance, central banks hold the monopoly over money. This empowers them to enforce an independent monetary policy that is supposed to serve the overall interests of the citizens and their government. At least, this is the general and noble intent.

The reality, however, is all too often different: the Cantillon effect, proposed by the British economist Richard Cantillon back in the 18th century, systematically favors some people over all others. When new money is created, banks and state-owned companies are always the first to profit. If asset and real estate prices rise as a consequence, those who can best access the stock and bond markets will in turn be better off than others.

Economic and societal distortions created by monetary policy are difficult to quantify, but they are very real after all. In his main treatise on economics, *Human Action*, published in 1949, Ludwig von Mises compared the market economy with a monetary democracy. Every monetary unit spent is like a ballot that goes toward deciding on the production structure within the economy. The creation of money distorts this "voting process" and manipulates it to a certain extent, but it usually goes unnoticed by the general public.

The power of existing ballots held by real consumers and savers is weakened this way. It is no longer they who decide on the production structure of the economy but instead, indirectly, the actors behind money creation, such as central and commercial banks. This monetary policy has so far been without an alternative, and people have had to accept it. Until now.

With what can be called "strong assurances," Bitcoin and public blockchain networks have set themselves the goal of changing this state of constant distortions and lack of alternatives. In simple terms, "strong assurances" means that "the rules are the rules," which will be enforced in a stringent and objective way. If someone does not approve of how these "strong assurances" are set up, they can opt out of the blockchain network. Forking makes that possible by allowing the software code of a public blockchain to be copied at any time and continued elsewhere under a new name. In so doing, disagreements can be solved in a way that is not possible in the world of physical objects.

Forking Makes It Possible

The concept of forking comes from the field of open-source software (OSS). In contrast to so-called proprietary (i.e., copyrighted) software, developers do not have to develop completely new products, but can copy and modify the existing program code and publish a new variant of the program. Each new version is a descendant of the previously developed code, but it is independent and unique. Forking is a constant phenomenon in the field of open software. Since blockchains are ultimately software, they can also go through forks. Blockchain forks are typically divided into the categories of "soft fork" and "hard fork." A soft fork is any change to the source code that is backward compatible. If, for example, a blockchain whose blocks were previously 1 megabyte in size switches to block sizes of 500 kilobytes, it is a soft fork. The new rule does not conflict with the old one, since 500 kilobytes are less than 1 megabyte. The network still accepts the new blocks.

In contrast, a hard fork denotes a protocol change that is not backward compatible. For example, if the block size is increased from 1 to 2 megabytes. The hard fork extends the rules in a way that the network can no longer fulfill them—and a split occurs.

The following is a good analogy to illustrate these splitting scenarios: Imagine that a blockchain is a large restaurant that is run collectively. There is no central authority that can alone enforce decisions. In the beginning, the restaurant serves only vegetarian dishes. If the chefs decide to cook only meat dishes from now on, it would be like a hard fork. Previous customers must either accept these meat dishes or look for a new restaurant. On the other hand, a soft fork would occur if the cooks decide to opt for a completely vegan kitchen. In this case, vegetarians could continue to visit the restaurant.

Bitcoin has already experienced several soft and hard forks. Satoshi Nakamoto even implemented early soft forks himself through one-sided software upgrades. The 2017 Segregated Witness (or SegWit) update was probably one of Bitcoin's most famous soft forks. This was crucial because it created many new opportunities for Bitcoin's technical development. This is also the time when Bitcoin Cash, the most prominent hard fork, split off from the original Bitcoin Core protocol (more about this in chapter 18).

At first glance, blockchain forks seem rather suspect. After all, they seem to offer the possibility of creating values out of thin air. However, those who pay a little more attention to the phenomenon realize that forks are a socio-evolutionary mechanism of public blockchain networks that make it possible to try out new ideas and solve conflicts.

Obviously, an excess number of forks is not advantageous for a public blockchain network. With each splitting, there is a division of the mining capacity provided by miners, also called hash power. The more it "dilutes" and spreads over individual forks, the less secure each individual version becomes. It therefore makes the most sense for as many miners as possible to gather on a single version and carry out their mining work there.

In order for a fork to be successful, it must convince exponents of the old community to follow along. Only if enough users, developers and miners turn to this fork can it survive in the long run. This is where the aforementioned "strong assurances" come into play by attempting to convince users to follow the hard fork rather than remain with the old network. And since a spin-off exists as a new project independent of the old one, there is no inflation of assets within the old network. Accusing Bitcoin of being inflationary and having no value because many Bitcoin forks and other altcoins have been created is like saying that gold has no value because there are various other precious metals being dug up.

To this day, forks of popular cryptocurrencies often increase in value. This may be because network effects in the crypto world still don't seem to take full effect; even projects with few users continue to live on. In the long run, however, it is expected that one version will prevail and all others will disappear. In the case of Bitcoin, forks like Bitcoin Cash, Bitcoin Gold and Bitcoin Diamond will most likely one day be history.

Exit or Voice

According to German-American economist Albert O. Hirschman, participants in a network basically have two options for reacting to a deterioration in quality: they can leave (exit) or work from the inside toward an improvement (voice). This can also be seen in conventional systems: citizens of a country either emigrate or protest against oppression; dissatisfied employees quit their jobs or go on strike; customers shop elsewhere or call on the manager to insist on improvements. Whether the exit or voice option is chosen is a question of costs, both financial and emotional.

As digital networks become more widespread, Hirschman's concept must be extended to include forks, which combine the exit and voice options and thus significantly reduce the costs of both.

Open-source projects are becoming more and more popular. However, they often fail due to a lack of funding. While companies can market their proprietary solutions and thus generate revenue for new developments, the open-source community has had to rely on itself, with support from foundations or donations.

With the emergence of commercial blockchains such as Bitcoin and Ethereum (discussed in more detail in chapter 13), the incentive structures within the open-source world have changed for the better. By allowing the independent exchange of value through blockchain protocols, developers can be more easily rewarded for their work by the community.

Developments like the Lightning Network, which allows micropayments of a few cents over the internet (more on this in Chapter 19), should bring further improvements to developers' personal finances. Five cents from a single person is negligible, but when hundreds of thousands of enthusiasts pay five cents each, the sums become considerable. This creates incentives for developers to remain innovative and receptive to feedback (voice), rather than programming past users' needs. Like the sword of Damocles, the possibility of being forked by other developers hangs over the heads of programmers and spurs them on.

Thanks to these developments, the gap between proprietary and license-free innovation is likely to get smaller and smaller, with success and prevalence shifting further in favor of the latter. Proprietary systems that already compete with each other will not be able to compete with the infinitely large resource pool of public systems in the long run.

Microsoft, the world's largest software developer, admitted this fact in May 2019 by integrating Linux into the Windows operating system. Over the past few years, Linux has evolved from a small open-source project to the most common operating system for web servers and now supports Android, the world's most popular mobile operating system. If Linux is so successful as an open-source project, how much more can we expect from public blockchain networks for which incentives for innovation are even higher?

Anthropologist David Graeber defines "bullshit jobs," in his book of the same name, as an occupation that is so meaningless, unnecessary or harmful that even the worker cannot justify its existence. Such jobs make no meaningful contribution to society. In search of the opposite, namely meaningful work, more and more programmers are likely to turn to crypto networks and their seemingly endless possibilities.

THE CRYPTO WAR
NOW THEY CAN EVEN PAY WITH THIS BITCOIN?! ARGHHH!!!
ONE OF US MUST HAVE FINANCED THIS! THERE IS NO OTHER EXPLANATION!
WASN'T ME!
UHH...
IT'S TIME WE MAKE A MOVE!
WE'LL START WITH THE MEDIA!

Bitcoin is resilient. Bitcoin is principled. Bitcoin is native to internet ideals. And it's a great brand.

Jack Dorsey, CEO Twitter

11. The Supremacy of Permissionless Innovation

It was with Facebook's announcement to launch a cryptocurrency, called Libra, that many mainstream people started to wonder: Might there be something to this crypto thing after all? Others were reassured of their opinion that cryptocurrencies could only be shady given that Facebook, with its bad reputation as a violator of people's interests, was going crypto. Nevertheless, Facebook and its plans for Libra certainly achieved one thing: it pushed the topic of cryptocurrencies on to a whole new level of discussion.

With Libra, the debate on money has been complicated further. The state's monopoly over money is not only being attacked by non-centralized money like Bitcoin, but is being challenged by the existence of corporate currencies as well. What seemed to be unthinkable just a few decades ago is now turning into reality: government, enterprise and the internet are fighting over optimal money.

Facebook is really the first company to make a serious attempt at launching private corporate money again, after privately issued money had been a thing in the 19th century in countries like Scotland, Canada and Switzerland. Well aware of its rather bad standing with the general public, the tech giant has assembled a consortium called the Libra Association to oversee the project. In order to achieve decentralization, different members of the association are to be geographically dispersed across the planet, and no single member is to have more than 1 percent of the votes—not even Facebook itself.

For its global headquarters, the Libra Association has chosen to settle in the city of Geneva, Switzerland, presumably due to the country's openness toward the crypto and blockchain sectors (more on this in chapter 12). As its main product, the association is set to launch a wallet called Calibra, which would be integrated with Facebook Messenger and WhatsApp—applications with over 1.7 billion users around the world combined. In order to ensure the separation of social and financial data, Calibra is to be built as a regulatory subsidiary.

On the more technical side, the Libra protocol is structured as an open-source project, allowing all sorts of developers to read, build and provide feedback. This open-source protocol is called Libra Core, which will power the new Libra Blockchain network. The latter will use Merkle trees and a Byzantine fault tolerance (BFT) consensus protocol, both of which are components of blockchain technology. Nevertheless, Libra will use neither blocks nor a chain, but rather a single data structure that records the history of transactions and states over time.

The Libra network is referred to as a permissioned blockchain (more on this in chapter 9), which means that it is not open for anyone to run a node. The founding members of the association must pay $10 million up front to become validating nodes. In that sense, Libra's consensus mechanism resembles a proof-of-stake algorithm (more on this in chapter 21).

A New Macro Force

Tech giants like Facebook, Amazon and Apple have long been identified as a potential disruptive force to the financial sector. Now that the social media platform is trying to take such a concrete step forward in this regard, things are getting even more interesting. In the media, Libra is portrayed to be an outright threat to traditional banks. In terms of Libra's potential to reach customers through Facebook, the projected possibilities are endlessly greater than those of the biggest banks, such as J.P. Morgan, Citibank and Goldman Sachs. If every Western bank customer were to shift just 10 percent of their bank savings into the Calibra wallet, its reserve fund would become a major force in the global bond market, valued at over $2 trillion USD. Traditional banks would see the deposits of their customers shrink—a sort of modern-day bank run instigated by Libra.

While public statements from bankers about Facebook's project are rather rare, economists, politicians and technocrats have turned their attention toward Libra. The United States House of Representatives Committee on Financial Services has even addressed Facebook directly, confronting them with their concerns about the Libra project. Furthermore, in letters issued by public officials of the U.S. Congress, members of the Libra Association were asked to turn their backs on the project.

And lo and behold, about three months after Libra's initial announcement, PayPal, Visa, Mastercard, Stripe, eBay, Mercado Pago and Booking Holdings backed out of the association, leaving it with 21 members including Uber, Lyft, Spotify and Vodafone. Many have taken this as a clear sign that the project will be buried before it will have officially started.

In a mixture of indignation and malicious joy, Bitcoiners in particular point out the fact that the mother of all cryptocurrencies does not have an address to which such threatening letters can be sent, highlighting the true strength of permissionless innovation. And indeed, Bitcoin is non-central. It's for the reasons that Libra is demonstrating firsthand that Satoshi Nakamoto has reduced Bitcoin's possible attack surface to a minimum (more on this in chapter 1).

Libra, on the other hand, has enough points of contact, which is why there are warranted doubts about whether or not it is a true cryptocurrency. Paradoxically, the fact that Facebook has been showcasing its Libra token as an application of blockchain technology and advertising the project using terms typically associated with cryptoassets—such as *nodes*, *stablecoin* and *permission-free*—has no technical basis. As Tencent has already impressively shown with WeChat in China, digital peer-to-peer payment is very possible and easily doable without having to use either a blockchain or a cryptocurrency.

Exploiting the Regulatory Niche

The reason why Facebook has labeled Libra as a cryptocurrency is of a regulatory nature. The crypto sector is still more or less a vaguely regulated area—and due to its global reach and digital nature, this is likely to remain so in the foreseeable future. The people behind Facebook and Libra have cleverly anticipated this: if they want to have any chance of success with Libra, they will need to exploit the advantages of today's crypto world. For example, the clever minds behind Libra may consider outsourcing the almost-insurmountable KYC and AML requirements that a project of this size entails to crypto trading exchanges and thus to third parties—a strategy that is only conceivable in this new world of the blockchain. As a matter of fact, the new digital crypto space offers many more loopholes to further one's business, a circumstance the Libra Association is eager to profit from.

As is obvious, the U.S. political elite cannot and will not tolerate such audacity; as such, the reactions of U.S. politicians have been and continue to be grim. However, the arrogance and lust for power with which they badmouth the Libra project seem rather grotesque. Will U.S. bureaucrats, technocrats and functionaries soon put a final nail in Libra's coffin?

But sooner or later, U.S. politicians might discover this endeavor, which they are very much against today, to be something of an unexpected blessing. One of the most important aspects of Libra is the fact that its token is designed to be stable in terms of price. To achieve this, the token will be fully backed by a fund of reserve assets, which, apart from imminent liquidity in the form of cash, will consist of government bonds from a wide range of first-world nations. In the style of a private central bank, a group of managers will oversee Libra's reserve fund to ensure the price stability of the Libra token. If the demand for Libra increases, new Libra tokens will be issued and the reserve fund will be further supplemented with new government securities. This way, the appreciation of Libra is weakened. Opposite moves will be undertaken if demand for Libra tokens slackens; securities from the reserve fund will need to be sold on the open market for the Libra token to stabilize its price.

Geopolitical Weapon

Interestingly enough, half of all the securities in the Libra reserve basket are to consist of short-term U.S. government bonds. The rest is to be made up of government bonds in euros, yen, pounds sterling and Singapore dollars. Thus, demand for Libra is ultimately a demand for U.S. government bonds—a fact that the U.S. should consider as quite an argument in favor of Libra.

It is this argument that could slowly sway U.S. politicians toward Libra, once they discover how exactly the project could play in their hands. After all, Libra is targeting the masses of people who are unlikely to be invested in U.S. debt securities today, including people without access to credit institutions and asset managers. Targeting these groups is also the reason why Facebook has made sure that NGOs like Kiva and Women's World Banking are on board the Libra Association. So if the unbanked are able to hold just a portion of their savings in Libra tokens, this could open the door for them to participate in today's global economy. Indirectly, they would also become part of our financialized world by having their third-world savings channeled into first-world debt securities. Some critics thus describe Libra to be a monetary colonialism. While this statement seems to be harsh, it is not unlikely that the U.S. government could benefit the most from such a dynamic.

Libra as a geopolitical tool of the U.S.? It stands to reason that in the foreseeable future, we will see the U.S. establishment making a turnaround on the question of Libra. The politicization of the financial markets is progressing. Various means are being used by different players to steer international capital flows in their respective favor. For example, the European Union has recently issued regulations that make it more difficult for European investors to buy exchange-traded funds (ETFs) domiciled in the U.S. Anyone who talks to European asset managers quickly learns about the fact that it is becoming increasingly difficult to acquire securities denominated in U.S. dollars.

But such regulations are unlikely to leave the U.S. cold. The Libra project is well suited to become a geopolitical weapon. Once Libra is launched and becomes widespread in Europe due to the many people using WhatsApp, the European Union's only option would probably be to take a stand against Libra. The U.S. could then call Europe an enemy of innovation, maneuvering itself offside with a defensive stance on technology yet again. And not only that, Libra could also become a crucial tool in fighting for supremacy with China over blockchain technology. At the end of October 2019, Chinese President Xi Jinping definitely kicked off the race with his very positive and committed statements regarding the new world of blockchain.

The U.S. has not yet seemed to have recognized this clever strategy. But perhaps the idea of embracing Libra at some point is already in the minds of astute U.S. politicians who, with their current tirades, only want to make sure the government's weight and say in the Libra project will be greater than what it seems to be today.

A PIECE OF THE PIE
IN ASIA
HOW CAN WE REGULATE SOMETHING WE DON'T UNDERSTAND?
LET'S JUST FORBID ALL CRYPTOS!
HEY! THIS BITCOIN THING IS GOING THROUGH THE ROOF! IT'S CURRENTLY TRADING AT 15'000 U.S. DOLLARS.
HMMM... MAYBE WE SHOULD ALSO START INVESTING!
WHAT ARE YOU DOING WITH THOSE MACHINES IN THE VAULT?
WE'LL START MINING DIGITAL GOLD! BUT PSSST, KEEP THIS TO YOURSELF!
A FEW DAYS LATER, AT HERBERT'S OFFICE
TODAY IT ROSE TO 19'000 U.S. DOLLARS! THIS CAN'T BE
AND THE CENTRAL BANKS JUST LET THIS SLIDE!? WE NEED MUCH STRONGER REGULATIONS!
...NOW THE ASIAN REGULATORS REIGN.
ANIMUS DOMINI*!
*TO ASSERT SOVEREIGNTY.

We want to actively participate in the opportunities blockchain technology creates. Especially the creation of a new asset class seems very promising.

Martin Keller, CEO Falcon Private Bank

12. The Diverse World of Cryptoassets

Bitcoin and the wider crypto scene are a global phenomenon. Public blockchain networks are controlled neither by a state nor by a company. Rather, they connect the most diverse people across national borders.

Yet despite all this non-centrality, some states—Switzerland, above all—are trying to create points of contact with national interests and jurisdictions. At the beginning of 2018, former finance minister Johann Schneider-Ammann announced "Crypto Nation Switzerland." He urged universities, industry and government to make this small country into one of the world's most important crypto hubs. Many crypto visionaries and blockchain enthusiasts considered this a clever move.

Schneider-Ammann was recognizing, after the fact, that Switzerland had already become a real hotspot for the new technology. According to the consulting firm PwC, in 2017, $1.46 billion USD were invested in 33 different ICO projects (more on this in chapter 6), primarily in the canton of Zug, the Swiss "Crypto Valley." Four of the six largest ICOs worldwide took place in Switzerland. FINMA, the Swiss Financial Market Supervisory Authority, was the world's first regulator to issue guidelines on ICOs.

With its guidelines on token classification, it created a framework that provided a topic of discussion worldwide. As the Swiss regulator correctly recognizes: not all tokens are the same. For example, one type of token assumes the function of a currency. As in the case of bitcoin, and in contrast to conventional, national fiat currencies, this token is not issued by a central bank but is created by the act of mining by different actors involved in the system. As a reward, coins are newly minted. In its statement, FINMA described this type of token as a payment token.

Before the arrival of cryptoassets, a token was usually understood to mean a voucher, coupon or ticket, such as an admission to a film. FINMA refers to tokens in this context as utility tokens. Outside of certain scenarios, they have little value.

The third and last type defined by FINMA is the asset token. Also known as security tokens, these are connected to some sort of backing and are subject to a redemption obligation. For example, they can take the form of equity tokens, a kind of digital share, or can be backed by real estate. Through a smart contract, a self-executing contract on the blockchain, dividends can be paid to the equity token holders—in a cryptocurrency, of course. As with shares, the holders can participate in voting, which is executed transparently through the blockchain.

The FINMA guidelines gave a big boost to the professionalization of the token world. Some banks then began to address this new phenomenon. Meanwhile, all sorts of executives, investors and politicians started trying to make a name for themselves in this field. Many congratulated each other on having established the Crypto Nation Switzerland. But a healthy dose of humility would serve them well: they adorn themselves with laurels that they have neither planted nor really cared for themselves.

Innovation Bottom-Up

The fact that Switzerland has a respectable crypto scene today is mainly due to the commitment of a small number of private individuals. Around 2011, a few computer enthusiasts and anarcho-libertarians began to take an interest in the new phenomenon for technical and ideological reasons. In the early days, their attention was focused on Bitcoin—after all, there were no other cryptoassets as of yet. Switzerland's first crypto startup was called Bitcoin Suisse AG, and the first crypto and fintech association was Bitcoin Association Switzerland. They did pioneering work and were even able to poach some well-connected heavyweights from the traditional Swiss banking world.

An important milestone in the development of the Swiss crypto scene was the decision of the Ethereum Foundation to settle in Zug. Ethereum, the second-largest public blockchain after Bitcoin, had a strong pull effect. More and more clever minds sought proximity to the Ethereum community and used their blockchain as a platform. At the same time, they benefited from networks of developers and investors that were established in Zug and other Swiss cantons.

The fact that Ethereum had opted for Switzerland and not Singapore was explained by the fact that Switzerland, with its confederalist structure, would best reflect the idea of decentralization underlying the crypto movement. Authorities in Switzerland are perceived to be much more approachable than in a centrally managed country—and the bureaucracies can be reasoned with. Crypto enthusiasts from all over the world therefore regard the cantonal authorities as cooperative service providers who do not see startups as merely annoying petitioners.

Another important reason that attracted many crypto proponents to Switzerland from the very beginning is the flexible Swiss legal system, which makes it possible to apply existing laws—which tend to be generic and broadly encompassing, and thus widely applicable—to the new challenges with little effort. Tax and other financial law questions can be answered more quickly in Switzerland than in, for example, the EU.

There are historical reasons for this. In 1848, the Swiss federal state began as a minimal state. In the early days there was only a handful of professional civil servants, no taxes and a minimum budget fed by customs duties. These structures, however, arose less from the commitment to a "lean state" than from the fact that the means for more than a minimal state were simply not available. One had to be pragmatic.

Perhaps this is precisely the reason why relatively many people in Switzerland are convinced of blockchain technology's potential and are using it to breathe new life into the Swiss financial industry, which is in dire straits. It suffered greatly from the financial crisis of 2008 and the subsequent tightening of regulations. Between 2007 and 2017, the financial sector's contribution to the Swiss GDP fell from 8.2 percent to only 4.6 percent.

At the beginning of 2019, the crypto industry in Switzerland and Liechtenstein already counted over 750 companies. Five of these crypto projects, which originate in Switzerland or are rooted there, even belong to the herd of so-called unicorns: Bitmain, Cardano, Xapo, Dfinity and Ethereum have a value of $1 billion USD or more.

For a long time, the canton of Zug seemed to be the heart of the Swiss crypto scene. In particular, Crypto Valley Labs, which opened in 2017, further increased the international attractiveness of the location. The Zug-based blockchain consulting firm Lakeside Partners was renamed Crypto Valley Venture Capital (CV VC) in 2018. Over the next five years, between $50 million $100 million USD are to flow into emerging crypto startups via this channel.

In 2018, Trust Square, Zurich's first blockchain hub, opened its spaces on the expensive Bahnhofstrasse. Right next to the Swiss National Bank and not far from Paradeplatz, the symbolic center of the traditional Swiss banking world, several dozen Blockchain startups are quartered here—from a one-man project to a young company with over 50 employees. In order to make the public more aware of what is happening in the Swiss Blockchain sphere, Trust Square strives for intensive cooperation with local authorities.

The crypto scene also works closely with universities. Intensive research is being conducted on blockchain-related issues at the Swiss Federal Institute of Technology (ETH) Zurich, the University of Zurich and the University of Applied Sciences Rapperswil. Within the framework of its Center for Innovative Finance research unit, the University of Basel has been holding blockchain lectures for a number of years, combining economics, computer science and cryptography in an interdisciplinary manner.

A Contradiction

Switzerland is a good example of how a state and non-central business models can cooperate and benefit from each other. While the crypto world develops new projects with state support and sometimes even financing, the battered Swiss banking and financial sector is hopeful that it can continue to exist without banking secrecy and prosper again in the not-too-distant future through the innovations of Crypto Valley.

At this point, this might be sounding alarm bells among readers. The crypto world has set out to establish a non-central financial system beyond state control. What is happening in Switzerland is diametrically opposed to this idea. The manifold blockchains developed in Zug, Zurich and elsewhere may advance the technology, create jobs and benefit Switzerland's reputation as an innovative country, but they betray the sometimes slightly crypto-anarchist foundation on which the crypto world is based.

What can be done about this? Crypto enthusiasts of the first hour now have to endure these contradictions that accompany the increasing professionalization and monetarization of their sphere. Or, with the belief that this is a competition of systems and ideas, try to stand their ground, whether worldwide or in a niche.

A look at the conventional market economy illustrates the choices. After all, it consists not only of large profit-driven corporations, but also entrepreneurs and organizations that do not strive for profit at all. For example, Wikipedia, the online encyclopedia, is not profit-oriented, yet it ranks fifth among the most visited websites in the world because it offers an added value that a purely commercial company could never offer.

Similar processes of consolidation versus differentiation are likely to continue to occur in the crypto world in the coming years. Thanks to clever location promotion, Swiss companies will be at the forefront—whether all crypto supporters welcome it or not.

THE BIGGEST MEETUP
...AND THIS IS HOW BITCOIN WILL CHANGE OUR WORLD!
ANDREAS, I HAVE A QUESTION!
WHAT IS THE INTRINSIC VALUE OF A BITCOIN?
HOW IS IT CALCULATED?
IS BITCOIN COMPARABLE TO MONEY OR GOLD?
...ANOTHER QUESTION: WHY IS IT SO VOLATILE?
BITCOIN IS THE INTERNET OF MONEY.
IT'S A NEW PHENOMENON. NOT EVERYONE HAS UNDERSTOOD IT.
THIS IS WHY IT'S SO VOLATILE!
INTERESTING!

There is this broader subculture of people trying to make libertarian tax havens of different levels of extremeness. I think one of the problems of libertarian tax havens and libertarian havens in general, both online and offline, is that they attract both people who like freedom and rich people who are not particularly interesting.

Vitalik Buterin, Inventor of Ethereum

13. The Rise of Ethereum

When the crypto market reached a capitalization of about $800 billion USD in January 2018, many enthusiasts excitedly talked about a Bitcoin revolution. But with the collapse of its price, euphoria vanished and the revolution was postponed. Only a few hardcore Bitcoiner acknowledged that the crypto world has nevertheless already achieved something unique: with Bitcoin, the first digital bearer instrument was created, a digital asset that can be used independently and self-sovereignly.

And it is even more than that. "Bitcoin is the first example of a new form of life," wrote Ralph Merkle, a pioneer in the field of asymmetric cryptography. "It lives and breathes on the internet. It lives because it can pay people to keep it alive […] It can't be changed. It can't be argued with. It can't be tampered with. It can't be corrupted. It can't be stopped […] If a nuclear war destroyed half of our planet, it would continue to live, uncorrupted."

Bitcoin may be the first life-form of this new kind, but it is no longer the only one. Above all, another blockchain project has cast a similar spell over people all over the world: Ethereum. From July to August 2014, the Ethereum Foundation, based in Zug, Switzerland, conducted an initial coin offering (more on ICOs in chapter 6). Owners of bitcoin could exchange them for ether, the token within the Ethereum network, and thus invest in the vision of today's second-largest cryptoasset.

The first difference between the two networks is readily obvious: while Bitcoin has grown without official fundraising, Ethereum was initiated in the style of an investment project. As we will see below, this is essential to Ethereum's nature and further development.

The World Computer

The mastermind behind Ethereum is Vitalik Buterin. At the tender age of 17, the Canadian with Russian roots came across Bitcoin through his father. The crypto project fascinated him, and Buterin began to dig his head into it more and more. In his eyes, Bitcoin was an impressive piece of programming code, but hardly anyone developed applications on top of it. Buterin wanted to improve on this supposed limitation of Bitcoin.

From the point of view of Bitcoin developers, however, this limitation was intended. Since the conception of the Bitcoin blockchain, its main task has been to enable the most secure way of exchanging digital value. In order not to endanger this goal, Bitcoin was programmed in a script language that is as rudimentary as possible but all the more robust.

Buterin saw it differently. For him, one thing was certain: in order for developers to be better able to program new software on the Bitcoin protocol, a more complex script, a so-called Turing-complete programming language, would be needed. Such a language can be used to execute programs of any complexity.

However, critics countered Buterin's approach by saying that this would increase the susceptibility to errors. When he was unable to convince the Bitcoin community of his concern, he put his ideas into practice independently and connected with others who shared his vision. After its code had been programmed and its ICO had flushed bitcoin and government fiat currencies worth $18 million into its coffers, the first Ethereum block was created on July 30, 2015.

Buterin describes Ethereum as a kind of world computer—and according to his idea, the blockchain is exactly that. It exists as a non-centralized hard disk on which all events, transactions and interactions happening on the blockchain are stored as a state, as it is called in computer science. They can then be retrieved by the computer network and processed synchronously.

In fact, Bitcoin is already a world computer, the world computer par excellence. By mid-2019, the 500 most powerful supercomputers in the world together accounted for just 1.6 percent of the performance potential of the Bitcoin blockchain. However, this high performance is not used for transaction throughput but flows primarily into security, which is why the Bitcoin blockchain is way more secure than any other computer network in the world (more on this in chapter 18). The fact that the analogy of the world computer is mainly used in the context of Ethereum, however, has to do with the fact that any applications can be programmed on it.

Like Bitcoin, Ethereum is based on a public blockchain. By mid-2019, the Ethereum network was distributed among approximately 9,000 computers around the world that communicate with each other via the Ethereum protocol. Due to its non-central structure, the Ethereum world computer can be manipulated only with extreme effort. In addition, such a world computer is extremely robust due to its redundancy. The Ethereum "hard disk" does not exist only in one place but is distributed all over the world. The risk of failure is therefore many times lower.

The Programmable Blockchain

In connection with Ethereum, the term *smart contract* is used again and again. The Ethereum blockchain is generally regarded as the blockchain project that first recognized the potential of such "intelligent contracts" and popularized the idea.

In the case of the Bitcoin blockchain, a primitive form of smart contracts is already used, and are limited to simple bitcoin value transfers. Since Ethereum is a programmable blockchain, its smart contract functions can be extended almost arbitrarily in theory. In addition to processing transactions of digital value, a smart contract can be used to transfer other sorts of values such as bonds, shares and other—sometimes even physical—property titles. The various contracts that we conclude every day can be converted into computer code, stored on the blockchain in the form of smart contracts and executed by the Ethereum network in a non-centralized manner—at least, this is the vision of Ethereum enthusiasts.

The elegance of a smart contract lies in the fact that it executes itself according to predefined parameters. If the contract conditions are fulfilled, the contract executes itself according to its terms: for example, the agreed product is delivered against payment. In addition, the smart contract not only defines the rules and sanctions relating to the agreement, but it also enforces them itself (more on the challenges in chapter 15).

Of course, it is ultimately the individual computers of the Ethereum network that execute the program code defined in a smart contract. These computers are also called Ethereum clients. Since Ethereum is Turing complete, the computers in the Ethereum network are capable of executing code of any complexity.

This requires computing power and energy in the form of "gas" paid for in ether. How much ether the gas costs depends on the current utilization of the Ethereum network. Not all smart contracts consume the same amount of gas. The more complex a contract, the more gas is needed for execution.

The users decide for themselves how much they want to pay for the gas. Depending on the set gas price, the initiated operation may or may not be given priority. With a future update called BASEFEE, this process will be automated, removing the need for each and every user to generate their own individual gas estimation strategy. A user will just have to press "Send Transaction," and the optimal market rate for gas will be calculate and processed for them.

Current gas (i.e., ether) recipients are the Ethereum clients or Ethereum miners—but this is likely to change in the foreseeable future (more on this in chapter 21). The higher the price is set, the greater the likelihood that the corresponding smart contract operation will actually be carried out, because Ethereum clients usually attend to the most lucrative offers. Even with the projected update through BASEFEE, users will still have the possibility to opt for a higher transaction fee, if they feel the need to have their transaction processed faster. As we have already learned, the execution does not take place endlessly, but only until the required amount of gas has been used up. No different from a vehicle, whose fuel tank becomes empty at some point.

Ethereum is now four years old and the second-largest cryptoasset in terms of market capitalization. In addition, Ethereum has become the de facto platform for crypto projects to raise funding through ICOs The enormous growth of the Ethereum community and its resulting dominance has led to the rise of other smart-contract platform projects.

Ethereum's Largest Competitor

The most prominent of these "Ethereum killers" is probably EOS, also called "Ethereum on Steroids" by some. In June 2018, following the largest ICO ever carried out on Ethereum, which generated a record sum of approximately $4 billion USD, EOS switched from an Ethereum-based token to its own blockchain, the EOS blockchain. Unlike Ethereum, the EOS consensus mechanism is based on "delegated proof of stake," or DPoS for short. This type of consensus-finding mechanism was invented by EOS founder

Dan Larimer. DPoS entitles every EOS token holder to elect the network's validators. One token, one vote. So those with more EOS tokens have a greater influence on the election result.

The validators mentioned above are block producers, who produce EOS blocks in mutual agreement, check their correctness and thus maintain the functionality of the blockchain. EOS token holders choose a total of 21 block producers, who are rewarded with new EOS tokens for their work. If a block producer does a poor job, validating invalid transactions, for example, they can be stripped of their status as a block producer. Voting takes place automatically about every two minutes.

In principle, it is therefore possible to change validators every few minutes. In addition to the 21 active block producers, there are about 100 more in standby mode. If one producer is deselected, another one moves out of the reserve.

Interestingly, no transaction fees are planned for EOS, since the EOS founders regard them as a hindrance. In Ethereum, miners who validate transactions and add them to the blockchain are currently remunerated for this service with transaction fees and 2 ether, which make up the so-called block subsidy. EOS block producers, on the other hand, receive newly created EOS tokens.

Each year, an additional 5 percent of EOS tokens are produced, which means that the stock is inflated annually by 5 percent. Of this 5 percent, 1 percent is divided up as a reward for each of the block producers for validating the transactions. The remaining 4 percent is placed in a separate pool, which will finance the further development of the EOS blockchain. EOS ensures that block producers cannot share their earnings with those who voted for them—votes therefore cannot be bought in this system.

In order to ward off attacks on the EOS blockchain, the bandwidth is dependent on the possession of the EOS tokens. If you own 1 percent of all tokens, you are entitled to 1 percent of the entire bandwidth of the network. In order to overload the network in a targeted manner, an attacker must buy EOS tokens. Spam attacks are therefore not ruled out, but they are economically expensive.

If you want to develop a decentralized application (DApp) on Ethereum, you need the computing power of the Ethereum miner and pay for it via ether gas. EOS, on the other hand, is based on the ownership model: if you hold one thousandth of the EOS tokens, you also have one thousandth of the total computing power on the EOS blockchain. For example, if you need

10 percent of the total EOS computing power to host a DApp, you have to own 10 percent of the total EOS tokens. This model allows DApp developers to realistically estimate their hosting costs at any time.

A Nonexistent Fight

Which blockchain will prevail in the long run, Ethereum or EOS? All too often, investors who hope to find an answer to this question today focus on the minds behind the two projects, staging the competition of ideas as a duel between Vitalik Buterin and Dan Larimer. Some Ethereum supporters refer to Buterin's allegedly astronomically high IQ. The opposite side refers to Larimer's two other very successful crypto projects, BitShares and Steem.

Technically, the EOS blockchain is maintained by a comparatively small number of nodes. In the crypto world, which is committed to the decentralization of social structures, a blockchain concept with only 21 block producers naturally arouses suspicion. Is EOS even decentralized or do the 21 block producers form a cartel or even an oligarchy?

Just as it is for many supporters of Ethereum, decentralization is not an absolute value for some EOS exponents. Since upholding a decentralized network is always associated with costs, they argue, compromises must be made in order to achieve the goal of mass scaling a blockchain and with it the use of DApps. EOS is just decentralized enough to be able to scale. The fact that there are just 21 block producers stems from Larimer's previous experience with BitShares and Steem, his other DPoS systems. If necessary, the number can be changed immediately.

Other advocates of EOS do not consider the EOS blockchain to be any less decentralized than Ethereum. They point out that at Ethereum, three parties—so-called mining pools—account for more than 50 percent of the total computing capacity. Theoretically, these three players could join forces to successfully attack the Ethereum blockchain and double-spend transactions.

It's important to point out though: Mining pools might be centralized, but this doesn't mean that miners are centralized too. Mining pools don't directly own huge mining machines, but rather apply lots of individual computational power to mine blocks. As an analysis in May 2019 has shown: In order to achieve a successful attack, an attacker has to convince at least 4484 miners to cooperate. In other words: at least 4484 miners would need to act maliciously to overthrow the Ethereum network, not just 3 pools. However, 4484 top miners make up only 1.5% of all actual miners in the network. Meanwhile, the EOS network is accused of having blocked EOS accounts several times—another sign, of course, that EOS is in a bad light when it comes to decentralization. As well, block producers are said to have reversed transactions that had already been confirmed.

In addition to decentralization, the aspect of immutability is being hotly debated in the dispute between the Ethereum and EOS. Under the phrase "code is law," some community representatives argue that a public blockchain should never be changed retroactively, since such a blockchain, by definition, should be seen as unchangeable and therefore should not be manipulated. With Ethereum, these arguments have already been thoroughly debated within the framework of the DAO hack (more on this in chapter 24). Under the aegis of the Ethereum Foundation, it was decided that the blockchain would be split into Ethereum and Ethereum Classic via a hard fork.

In order to avoid such conflicts within the community and potentially threatening hard forks in the first place, the EOS project decided not to regard the code as inviolable. In the EOS white paper, the following lines are written: "Sometimes a smart contract behaves in an aberrant or unpredictable manner and fails to perform as intended; other times an application or account may discover an exploit that enables it to consume an unreasonable amount of resources. When such issues inevitably arise, the block producers have the power to rectify such situations."

The EOS founders argue that block producers intervene only in the event of errors. Skeptics, on the other hand, see a back door that makes abuse possible. That's why EOS is manipulable in principle and not an unchangeable smart-contract platform, they say. Interestingly enough, many EOS sympathizers have no problem at all with this verdict. It seems as though the EOS community consists more of people who prefer a certain amount of leeway to exert influence than a state of complete unchangeability.

So, Ethereum or EOS? The former surely seems to be in the pool position to become the de facto smart contract platform. But the competition is so fierce that people often forget that it is not necessarily just one smart-contract platform that will prevail. Not unlike operating systems, of which several exist simultaneously with Windows, Android, macOS and Linux, different smart-contract platforms should also be able to play out different strengths and special features and thus maintain their positions in the market.

THE INTIMIDATION

Fundamentally the way that Lightning works is it uses the blockchain as an arbiter. The blockchain is a court and actually kind of like the way that you have contracts in real life, where not every contract goes to court, you can transact thousands maybe even millions of times and then only settle the total balance to the underlying blockchain.

Elizabeth Stark, CEO Lightning Labs

14. A New Internet

The internet has shaped the past two decades like no other technological development. "The web has become a public square, a library, a doctor's office, a shop, a school, a design studio, an office, a cinema, a bank, and so much more," wrote Tim Berners-Lee, one of the inventors of the World Wide Web.

Whether at home or at work, the internet has become indispensable for most people. Precisely because it is so pervasive and without alternative, most people have no choice but to grudgingly accept that essential areas of cyberspace today are dominated by quasi-monopolistic offerings. Whether in communications, cloud computing, search engines, marketing or internet infrastructure—a few providers dominate ever larger parts of the virtual world. As a result, the virtual world is becoming more and more centralized.

The vision of the internet was a different one. Originally, it was a project by the U.S. Department of Defense to establish a communications network that would be immune to unforeseen events such as natural disasters or war. Therefore, geographic decentralization was chosen so that in the event of a partial failure of the system, the rest would still function.

Peer-to-peer network connections were used for this purpose. In this way, each computer could communicate with any other computer in the network without being dependent on a central computer to act as a coordinator. In addition to the military, the academic world in particular used the new communications technology to exchange scientific data and findings.

With further development, the commercialization of the internet also took its course. More and more tech enthusiasts, computer scientists and investors became excited about the decentralized, global technology and worked on its further development. Early on, the new phenomenon also attracted the interest of freedom activists who were particularly familiar with the field of cryptography. In the 1990s, they founded the cypherpunk movement with the aim of using the internet as a tool against progressive restrictions on freedom by the state and large corporations.

Preprogrammed Centralization

While the cypherpunks have created a non-central, anonymous refuge called the dark web using VPN servers and Tor browsers (more on this in chapter 29), the majority of the internet is now in centralist hands. That it has developed in this direction is no coincidence. Rather, this is buried in its DNA:

Today's World Wide Web is based on several protocols. These ensure that the individual computers and servers can communicate with each other. An internet protocol is comparable to a language. Just as vocabulary and grammar enable people to communicate, the protocols of the internet ensure the regulated exchange of data between computers all over the world.

ARPANET, a computer network developed under the auspices of the Massachusetts Institute of Technology (MIT) and the U.S. Department of Defense, was the first public application of two protocols essential to today's internet, the Transmission Control Protocol and the Internet Protocol, or TCP/IP. With each additional node that joined ARPANET, the network became stronger and the incentives greater to develop new technology that would make the growing network even more functional.

Additional network protocols were created to facilitate the exchange of data between nodes. The Simple Mail Transfer Protocol (SMTP) helps to send and receive emails, the File Transfer Protocol (FTP) to exchange and read files, and the Hypertext Transfer Protocol (HTTP) to structure and display web pages. HTTP, one of the best-known public protocols, finally transformed ARPANET into the World Wide Web we know today. To this day, it is the standard for computer communications at the application level of the internet. Without this and the other protocols, nothing would work.

In general, basic internet protocols are public and accessible to everyone. Anyone can develop further protocols or applications on this basis. But while basic protocols can hardly be monetized, applications can be sold for good money. This is where most of the value was created in the early days of the internet, until companies discovered that when users surf the internet, they leave behind a trail of data that reveals a lot about their attitudes, interests and habits.

This insight may have led to the birth of today's platform economy. In order to collect as much data as possible, companies created their own networks with the goal of keeping users in their own systems for as long as possible with various incentives and offers, most of which are free of charge.

Since then, more and more innovation and progress have taken place on individual platforms. Data and value creation management are in the hands of tech companies. They own the data. Today's internet does not know of autonomous, self-sovereign ownership possibilities. The closed-platform economies are becoming increasingly ginormous and, as intermediaries, are taking ever larger pieces of the cake.

The large platform operators not only generate vast amounts of data, but they have also cleverly nestled themselves in the valuable and essential value chains of the digital age. Amazon, Google and Microsoft together account for over 60 percent of all cloud storage services. If you want to store and make content available on the internet, you can hardly avoid these tech giants.

For example, all the movies and shows that can be seen on Netflix, the largest video streaming provider, are stored on the servers of their archrival, Amazon. The instant-messaging service Snapchat, on the other hand, relies on Google's services for cloud hosting. Approximately half of its revenue goes to the internet giant.

The tech giants also dominate the app stores and advertising business. And their financial strength is enormous as well: Apple, the leader, is sitting on cash reserves of over $285 billion USD; Microsoft, just under half that; and Alphabet, Google's parent company, about $100 billion. It is becoming increasingly common for investors to hoard the shares of internet giants as a kind of money substitute. Investors are complaining about an investment shortage due to low interest rates, but the tech sector seems to be one last refuge for them. Nevertheless, many investors are worried about the uncanny stock market dominance of Google, Amazon and the likes.

An Internet-Native Financial System

Although the internet is like an onion with many layers, the World Wide Web has lacked a monetary layer for years. Value could not be valued, stored or exchanged directly on the internet without the intermediation of traditional financial institutions.

Due to the creation of Bitcoin, the internet now has this layer and its own financial system. As a multilayer protocol consisting of the Bitcoin base layer and the Lightning Network as a second layer (BTC/LN), it joins other open network protocols such as TCP/IP. The BTC/LN protocol also enables communication between the various nodes—with the difference that it makes internet-native values exchangeable. And the Lightning Network allows a smooth, anonymous and almost instant exchange of small amounts of bitcoin (more on this in chapter 19).

According to blockchain enthusiasts, however, an internal financial system should not be the end of the road. Enter Ethereum, which has given new impetus to the narrative of the sovereign internet user. As we saw in the previous chapter, Ethereum's vision does not only concern the monetary level. Rather, the Ethereum blockchain is intended to initiate the transition from a systemically flawed web 2.0 to a new web 3.0, for which in particular the concept of self-sufficient identity is essential (more on this in chapter 28).

This web 3.0 should consist of a multitude of new protocols that replace traditional web technologies such as HTTP, AJAX and MySQL as building blocks for applications. So-called money protocols shall be only one part of the new Internet (more on this in chapter 18). In its entirety, the DNA of web 3.0 should enable users to control their own data in order to guarantee privacy in an open, non-censurable internet. The Ethereum world computer and other additional protocols such as Polkadot, Cosmos or Dfinity might one day serve as the basis for this true peer-to-peer internet, which would no longer be based on central servers and centralized companies and authorities, but enable direct data flow between individuals.

Some experts, however, argue that the existing problems of the internet can be solved without the use of blockchain technology. They argue that many approaches would function quite well without it, and that many of the ideas required for an open, peer-to-peer internet already existed before the invention of the blockchain and were completely independent of it. As examples, they cite asymmetric cryptography (more on this in chapter 24) as well as ideas around the semantic web, distributed hash tables and the InterPlanetary File System.

What the popularization of blockchains actually did is intensify the discussion around improvements to the existing internet. With the advent of blockchain technology, many programmers have gained new hope. This is why they speak of the dawn of blockchain computing. A fascinating area of this is the idea of non-centralized data storage, often summarized under the buzzword "decentralized storage." Today, data is stored on centralized servers, making them popular targets for hackers. In addition, centrally stored data can be more easily manipulated or censored.

And another aspect that spurs developers to work on non-centralized alternatives: As the internet grows, more storage is needed. Additional storage capacities are already available today: all the gigabytes to terabytes that are unused on smartphones, tablets and computers of private users.

BitTorrent and other peer-to-peer data exchange systems for music and video files have shown that a system can work where many users manage copies of a file and distribute them in fragments to other members of the network. But the biggest problem with such systems is that there are no real incentives for network participants to stay online and provide their own computing power when they don't want to download files themselves. Various blockchain projects are trying to remedy this—and thus build a new internet apart from Amazon, Apple, Google and Facebook.

CLOSED OR OPEN?
IN JAY'S OFFICE
HEY JAY! HAVE YOU EVER HEARD OF A PRIVATE BLOCKCHAIN?
NO, DOES THAT EVEN MAKE SENSE?
LET'S ASK EVA!
SAY EVA, WHAT IS A PRIVATE OR CLOSED BLOCKCHAIN?
SOUNDS LIKE RUBBISH!
NOT NECESSARILY.
...IN A CLOSED SYSTEM A PRIVATE BLOCKCHAIN CAN MAKE SENSE, BUT IT HAS MORE THE CHARACTERISTICS OF A DATABASE. HOWEVER, IT CAN INCREASE ITS EFFICIENCY AND IS EASIER TO CONTROL.
BUT ONLY THE PUBLIC BLOCKCHAIN IS TRULY REVOLUTIONARY!
I'LL BUILD MY OWN BLOCKCHAIN AND CONNECT IT WITH BITCOIN AS A SIDECHAIN!
AND WHO OR WHAT WILL BE YOUR VALIDATORS?!

Since decentralized systems like Bitcoin are a superior technology, people will accept them naturally. Currently, the technology is not yet scalable enough to meet future demand. But it's only a matter of time before it can.

Niklas Nikolajsen, Co-CEO Bitcoin Suisse

15. Smart Contracts and Their Applications

In this chapter, we will take a closer look at the concept of smart contracts. We've already learned that these are rule-based software and are executed automatically according to predefined parameters. In principle, they are based on if-then statements. This sounds rather banal at first but could have far-reaching consequences in the future.

Smart contracts can be used to automate contract enforcement. It is hoped that this will lead to increased efficiency and a sustainable reduction in transaction costs, especially today when these are partly artificially inflated. The idea of smart contracts has existed since the advent of the internet in the early 1990s, but only now, with the invention of the blockchain, can it really be put into practice.

As we saw in the previous chapter, the internet did not have its own currency for a long time. That has changed with Bitcoin. But what the World Wide Web still lacks is an independent and native legal system. And this is despite the fact that cyberspace is omnipresent today and exists across national borders. In political terms, the internet is a diffuse "net state" whose "inhabitants" are occasionally referred to as "netizens," or net citizens.

Without internet-native legal structures, netizens remain in a kind of original state, comparable with the state of nature that the English political philosopher and theorist Thomas Hobbes described in the 17th century as "the war of all against all." According to Hobbes, this state is characterized by a lack of trust due to constant uncertainty.

For the American jurist Anthony T. Kronman, "transactional uncertainty" constitutes the state of nature. Although a person can make a promise, they do not have to keep it if failure to do so brings them greater benefit. The U.S. economist Oliver E. Williamson describes such behavior as opportunistic. Without confidence-building mechanisms, such behavior is likely to occur again and again. There is no binding basis for trust.

This description applies quite well to today's internet; opportunistic behavior is omnipresent in cyberspace. To counteract this, attempts are being made to enforce the physical world's established legal principles in the digital domain as well. This has been repeatedly unsuccessful, not least because of different legal systems and standards worldwide. In other words, because the world does not have a common government and is "anarchic."

Different moral values, on which legal structures are based, also complicate the building of a uniform order of trust throughout the World Wide Web. Meanwhile, established reputation mechanisms fail because of the anonymity of users: anyone who wants to regain a perfect reputation only has to choose a new pseudonym in many cases—this is referred to as "whitewashing" and is often only a few clicks away on the internet.

Overcoming the Digital State of Nature

Smart contracts are met with such a great response because they offer a solution to the trust problem inherent in the internet—vehicles based on algorithms and program codes that execute themselves independently, creating trust. Nevertheless, they are no panacea.

Smart contracts are not legally enforceable today. This is both an advantage and a disadvantage. The contractual provisions laid down in a smart contract are enforced outside the law, outside the jurisdiction and without state arbitration bodies. Especially for countries with corrupt legal institutions, smart contracts represent a major step forward.

However, the strict rules and independent enforcement without a potential mediator also make smart contracts a challenge. The algorithms stubbornly execute the stipulated contractual conditions without any discretionary scope. It becomes particularly problematic if a smart contract contains programming errors—it then executes itself anyway and cannot be canceled.

In addition, bugs in the source code can allow a smart contract to be manipulated in favor of one of the parties. This is the reason why the "code is law" approach is also met with skepticism. Programming errors are, as it were, loopholes in the law that can be exploited—and quite legally. Programmers are still worried about how they should deal with this problem. On the one hand, recurring programming errors undermine the basis of trust created by smart contracts. On the other hand, it is just as untrustworthy if smart contracts are constantly declared non-binding retroactively. Smart contracts are unlikely to succeed in making lawyers completely obsolete. And where lawyers *are* omitted, they could be replaced by programmers, who interpret smart contracts for laypersons and check for potential pitfalls. For this reason, work is also being done on standardized templates and combinable sample solutions to simplify the use of smart contracts.

Bridge Between the Analog and the Digital

Today, when a large and legally complex thing such as a property changes hands, the parties rely on the services of an independent trustee to ensure that the deal is properly executed and that none of the parties feel cheated. In order for a smart contract to take the trustee's place and for the transaction to be completely digital, the item being sold must be tokenized. In other words, the deed of ownership must take the form of a genuine digital asset, also known as a digital bearer instrument (more on this in chapter 25).

Only when this is the case can the digital deed of ownership be managed by the smart contract; in the case of a purchase, it can be passed on as soon as the purchase price has been paid. The smart contract ensures that neither party releases its property too soon and therefore gets nothing because the other party does not follow suit.

Critics argue that in a world dominated by smart contracts, there must be confidence that a tokenized deed of ownership actually represents the underlying asset. It would be useless if digital tokens were exchanged by smart contract, but the house in the real world did not change hands. In order to build this bridge between the digital and analog worlds, a trustworthy third party is still needed. True disintermediation is therefore not a given, the argument goes.

This leads us to the oracle problem. Similar to the oracles of ancient Greece, an oracle in the digital world is a data provider. Because a smart contract has no knowledge of reality, an oracle informs it of whether its requirements have actually been implemented in the physical world, thus providing data for the smart contract to "act." Since an oracle controls the "inputs" to a smart contract, it essentially holds power over the smart contract's actions. If the oracle is compromised, so is the smart contact—and herein lies the oracle problem.

This problem cannot be dismissed, but solutions are currently being worked on. One way might be to decentralize the oracle. A smart contract would then receive the relevant data not only from one party, but also from many independent bodies, which makes misuse much more difficult. In addition, the further development of the internet of things, or IoT, should ensure that machines and computers will one day become so advanced that they will be able to exchange the necessary information independently. Communication between cars, houses and other goods should further mitigate the oracle problem (more on this in chapter 25) and make trade more efficient.

Linking smart contracts and public blockchains should also lead to improvements. In the physical world, if a contract is not adhered to or is deliberately manipulated, it is not always easy for an authority or mediator to restore the original contract or adjust it retroactively. A lot can be covered up, especially since facts are often subjective. A public blockchain, on the other hand, is secure and transparent. In the event of discrepancies or contradictions, it provides a factual history that can greatly facilitate resolution between the parties or the execution of proper penalties.

New Name Wanted

So far, we have completely ignored one field of application for smart contracts: the state and its bureaucracy. For all those areas that leave no room for discretion, such as issuing a passport, smart contracts are predestined. Quite a few tech enthusiasts therefore consider government bureaucracies to be an optimal field of application for this new technology.

The sociologist Max Weber already knew at the beginning of the 20th century that bureaucracies are inefficient in the economic sense because of their rigid, rule-bound nature. Their way of working is mechanistic and thus dehumanizing. Smart contracts are therefore bound to increase the efficiency of public authorities.

However, it should be kept in mind that today's civil servants are human and can be talked to, and in certain scenarios and cases of hardship, they are capable of compassion and mercy. If the human factor is banned from bureaucracy and replaced by algorithms, the scope for discretion and thus individual justice would probably be eliminated. So, smart contracts would likely only bring real improvement to the services of the state if the latter were relieved of their rigidity and harshness. But it could be stated—paraphrasing Vito Corleone, the main character in the famous film The Godfather—that government monopolies and authorities offer services that private individuals cannot refuse. A more efficient bureaucracy might be all the more efficient in exercising power and enforcing these ultimately coercive offers—would that really be to the advantage of the citizens?

We talked about smart contracts from the point of view of existing structures and fields of application. Finally, we should recall the words of U.S. economist Gordon Tullock: "We tend to forget that there is such a thing as technological progress in contracts. People discover new ways of making agreements, and over a period of time we obtain considerable benefit from this sort of technological progress."

He was referring to the human tendency to look at new technologies through the eyes shaped by current technologies. When the first cars appeared on the roads in the 19th century, they were initially known as horseless carriages. It was only with time that this means of transport became detached from the idea of horses and carriages.

Today, we also judge smart contracts through our experience with and perspective of current contracts and procedures. However, they are perhaps something completely different, something new, for which we still have to find a suitable term—and suitable fields of application.

ONCE UPON A TIME...
FOLLOW ME! I'LL TAKE YOU ON A JOURNEY INTO THE PAST.
WHERE ARE WE?
IN THE ERA OF THE INTERNET BOOM!
WHAT ARE THOSE BLOCKS?
WELL, THEY'RE ACTUALLY YOU! THOSE BLOCKS ARE FULL OF DATA THAT YOU'VE LEFT IN THE INTERNET.
OH! THEN THEY MUST BE FULL OF PERSONAL DATA!
...AND CAN BE MISUSED!!!
BLOCKCHAIN CAN TRULY HELP US REGAIN CONTROL OF OUR DATA. THE KEYWORD IS: SMART CONTRACTS!
SMART WHAT?

Thanks to the crypto area, we now have the option to choose between predefined decentralized digital money and currencies managed by politicians and central bankers.

Thomas Winkler, Chairman Hyperliquid

16. The World of Decentralized Finance

In chapter 14, Bitcoin was discussed as a new monetary layer for the internet. The BTC/LN protocol would serve as a new foundation on which a new, internet-native financial system could be developed. And it is already happening: different groups and companies are building various services on top of this monetary layer—spawning many wallet providers, payment processors and custody solutions. Most of the services revolve around the aspects of holding as well as transacting, both of which are two key functions that a monetary layer needs to fulfill.

For the Ethereum community, it is not enough to have a monetary layer in the form of the BTC/LN protocol to build services on top of—especially since these services are not entirely based on code and can therefore only be built in a somewhat permissioned and more centralized fashion. Ethereum is a programmable blockchain (more on this in chapter 13) and includes a state machine that lets money be programmed. Be it a wallet, custody solution or full-blown bank provider, Ethereum programmers are currently turning them into unstoppable protocols. While software has gobbled up media over the last decade, banks are next on the its menu card, eating the world—as famously expressed by Marc Andreessen—one industry at a time.

Ethereum folks acknowledge that Bitcoin's base layer is truly permissionless. But so is gold, they argue, which has been tragically seized by central banks around the world, drastically weakening its permissionless character. In their view, the same thing will happen to Bitcoin if the systems that leverage the value of cryptoassets are not permissionless. Bitcoiners, on the other hand, consider Ethereum's approach to be no solution at all since they regard Ethereum's base layer as way too centralized from the get-go, making it a rather bad option to base an entirely new financial system on. Besides this, the notions of unstoppable code and smart contracts are also being criticized for being far too risky (more on this in chapter 15).

Fundamentally, the divide comes down to conflicting visions of the world (more on this in chapter 20). Depending on which vision your own thinking relates more naturally to, you may find yourself siding with one project or the other. Both cryptonetworks are ultimately faced with trade-offs, which is why it might not be bad to have them both go forward in their pursuits.

Back in 2017, the ICO craze bootstrapped Ethereum's network and attracted the attention of many people who found their way into crypto. Although today's feelings about initial coin offerings are rather negative (more on this in chapter 6), they were the first permissionless money protocol to take off. With the development of many new decentralized finance (DeFi) applications, many more money protocols are coming into existence, allowing the progress of decentralized finance to pick up speed.

Interestingly enough, in the traditional banking world, there is currently a similar movement called Open Banking. Its goal of opening up and standardizing application programming interfaces (APIs) is supposed to turn the banking industry into an open data economy and by doing so foster a cooperative instead of competitive ecosystem. Some people within the crypto ecosystem are therefore already rephrasing the term *decentralized finance* as *open finance* while making this point: the crypto movement—in its correct form and interpretation—is open by design and definition, making open finance a perfect tool to achieve the goals of Open Banking.

A Money Lego Network

Currently, the world of open finance is exploding with numerous building blocks that can all be combined, making it possible to build on top of or alongside each other. The cryptoasset ether is being used as the movement's base money, serving as collateral to make many higher-layer money protocols possible, the most important being MakerDAO. As described in chapter 8, this protocol mimics a sort of decentralized central bank translated into code. Its primary goal is to provide a digitally native and therefore permissionless stablecoin called Dai. This stable currency encourages people to use DeFi applications by helping them make long-term calculations. Dai is permissionless just as ether itself is. It cannot be seized arbitrarily. For the DeFi world to stay true to its name and overall goal, it's crucial that its two main collateral assets are of a permissionless nature. Although fintech startups like Revolut and Robinhood are pushing traditional banks to rethink their business and pricing models, conventional banking and investing still have many moats. Because of record prices, brokerage commissions, currency conversion fees, stamp duties and more, barriers to entry are high, especially for people in emerging or third-world countries, as well as younger generations in the Western world. In this regard, DeFi could be a game changer since it tackles and tries to solve many of these problems.

But to keep its long-term competitive advantage over traditional banking, the DeFi world must preserve its permissionlessness and openness as key features. The more mainstream open finance becomes, though, the higher the pressure will be to have KYC and AML regulations set up—at least at the fringes, as is already the case with many popular crypto on- and off-ramps. With MakerDAO, the most popular DeFi project, the Ethereum community is currently facing one such issue as well: Right now, Dai can be collateralized using only ether. But MakerDAO is projected to initiate the multi-collateralization of its stablecoin, which could mean that stablecoins such as Tether or DGX and, with them, real-world assets like the dollar or gold could be used as collateral in tokenized form. Dai's collateral would then no longer be completely permissionless since tokenized real assets currently involve some trusted third party. This is why some people in the DeFi space are rather skeptical of these developments.

DeFi's Killer App

A perceived advantage that DeFi seems to have over the traditional world of finance is interest. Many consider this to be its killer app par excellence. After all, people have been asking for actual use cases of open public blockchains, and the various money protocols offering interest are definitely one of them. The most popular of them is called Compound, an open-source, autonomous protocol that brings borrowers and lenders to the system of open finance. As a smart contract, it essentially establishes money markets of various Ethereum-based assets; from different pools of these assets, the protocol algorithmically derives interest rates based on the supply and demand for a particular asset. In the traditional world, lenders and borrowers are connected through a trusted third party such as a bank. With Compound, they interact solely and directly with the protocol. In other peer-to-peer protocols, borrowers have to reach terms with the lender regarding the loan's maturity, interest rate and collateral, but in Compound, all of these terms are aggregated into overall borrowing costs and assigned by the protocol, calculated based on pure market forces.

In order to secure the platform, loans on Compound are backed by over-collateralizing them, similar to the concept of MakerDAO described in chapter 8. Borrowers must deposit cryptoassets into Compound's smart contract to increase their borrowing power. If one's borrowing power falls below a certain threshold, collateral is automatically sold to cover debt. To give Compound's smart contract additional flexibility, borrowers are able to borrow only a certain amount of the collateral staked. Exactly how much this is depends on the value of the collateral as well as its liquidity in the market.

Compound's flexibility is enhanced because it works like a liquidity pool. This means that lenders are not matched to specific borrowers but are combined into one big aggregated pool. This allows users to withdraw their cryptoassets anytime. To ensure liquidity can be maximized, Compound makes use of an algorithmic interest rate that incentivizes borrowers to repay as early as possible.

Compound can be utilized to earn interest on one's cryptoassets, but interestingly, there's also the option to use the protocol to short a specific token. As a trader, you can go on Compound, borrow the respective token, sell it on an exchange and profit from this trade. Previously, a trader would have needed to go through a centralized exchange such as BitMEX to do this. With Compound, this process can be done in an open and permissionless way using a money protocol. From the perspective of DeFi, however, Compound is not perfect. Its governance structure in particular is currently centralized. The listing of new cryptoasset markets, the updating of interest rates and oracle addresses are managed by centralized hands. But its developers and engineers are hoping to give the protocol over to a community- and stakeholder-controlled DAO in the future (more on the concept of a DAO in chapter 24).

Compound is only one of many DeFi projects offering a platform for lending and borrowing. The reasons why the number of interest-paying platforms and other decentralized financial services is exploding are manifold. The new world of crypto is fostering permissionless innovation, and its idealistic goals to change current systems for the better are attracting more and more people who seem to see no more meaning in mechanically functioning as a mere cog in the traditional system. Along with this, DeFi users could also be considered negative interest rate policy (NIRP) refugees escaping the zero-interest-rate trap snapping in several parts around the world. In the Western hemisphere, checking and savings accounts pay hardly any interest anymore. Sovereign bonds of countries such as Switzerland, Denmark, Germany and Japan have negative yields. Whoever holds such a bond at maturity is guaranteed a loss.

Because of fees and negative interest rates—for many institutional investors, interest rates are already negative not only in real but in nominal terms—savings are being depleted. More and more people are thus forced to speculate on the open market through the help of banks and asset managers. Obviously, the new world of DeFi is not for everybody, since handling cryptoassets, let alone DeFi investment rails, is still a very technical undertaking. Those willing to learn and get acquainted with this new space of open finance are offered nice returns on loans, ranging from 5 to 15 percent annually. And DeFi even offers the possibility of profiting from real-world assets like silver, gold, real estate or stocks through synthetic assets that track corresponding underlying assets.

What makes DeFi so powerful from a user's perspective is the fact that all the protocols can be connected to interact seamlessly. Aggregators like Argent and Zerion—mobile wallets—combine different protocols. In the case of Zerion, Dai can be borrowed through MakerDAO, lent out immediately on Compound for interest and, once the returns are generated, swapped into ether anytime using the decentralized exchange protocol Uniswap—all in one application. No intermediaries are involved, which is why cost savings are significant.

High Yield, High Risk

Opportunities are truly vast. However, high returns usually also imply high risks—this is no exception in the DeFi world. Arguments that state that the risks involved on decentralized lending platforms can be hedged through the use of derivatives need to be taken with a grain of salt: hedging in an efficient market does always incur costs. There is no free lunch.

Accordingly, some observers from the traditional sector of finance are quick to judge: the crypto loan market is yet another credit bubble that is expanding too rapidly and is headed for a burst. They cite the following indicators as reasons for a potential blowup: lax lending standards, lack of regulatory oversight, too many lenders chasing too few borrowers and overly aggressive risk-taking. Whether this DeFi credit loan market really will explode sometime in the near future can only be known after the fact. However, at that point, the crypto credit bubble would be different in one crucial aspect: lenders, creditors and investors would all have to foot the bill on their own—quite contrary to traditional markets for which central banks repeatedly step in to cover the losses.

Risks nevertheless persist. For example, the issue of centralization (i.e., governance risk) has been alluded to. Some of the DeFi projects are centralized to the core; others appear to be decentralized, but doubts remain under the surface. Decentralized and permissionless protocols often depend on centralized oracles as data feeds (more about oracles in chapter 15). Another obvious risk comes from potential smart contract vulnerability—while careful code audits and formal verification processes by reputable security firms can help detect bugs, no smart contract can ever be guaranteed completely safe and free from bugs because humans are fallible after all. In the DeFi world, this can be considered a significant problem since, unlike in the traditional world, the blockchain sector is pretty much built around the philosophy of keeping things immutable. Because of this ethos, reversing transactions to make up for losses is unlikely to be a viable option.

Potential pitfalls—be it smart contract bugs, insufficient collateral liquidation, liquidity bottlenecks or centralization risk—always have to be assessed on a project-to-project basis; no two DeFi ventures are alike. But some people not only highlight the risks but question the purpose behind DeFi altogether: Why give out loans to people who can over-collateralize the entire loan, which goes to show that they don't even need it in the first place? And as a borrower, why use the bitcoin you won't sell to get ether you don't want to sell either? For others, the answers to these questions are easy: as a believer in the long-term appreciation of cryptoassets, one does not want to spend them but will nevertheless use them as collateral to leverage one's position in order to gain more cryptoassets.

Some would even argue that the use of over-collateralization can also be seen as a way to build upon a healthy base layer that allows for decentralized debt at all. Only then can DeFi take the next step, which is already beginning to happen. As a matter of fact, concepts revolving around decentralized credit scoring in conjunction with digital identity solutions are already being discussed. This way, a functioning reputation market could evolve to make possible decentralized lending without 100 percent collateralization. No matter how things develop and eventually turn out, the DeFi space should be followed vigilantly.

VISITING THE GENIUS
IN THE "BLOCK CAVE"
I'D LIKE TO INTRODUCE YOU TO SOMEONE. HERE, HE CAN WORK ON HIS INVENTIONS IN PEACE.
HI EVA, WHO DID YOU BRING WITH YOU?
THIS IS SATOSHI!?
HAHA! NO, SORRY IT'S NOT!
WELL, THERE ARE THOSE THAT THINK I'M SATOSHI. HOWEVER, MY NAME IS NICK SZABO.
HE'S THE MASTERMIND BEHIND SMART CONTRACTS! HE CAN TELL YOU ALL ABOUT THEM AND ANSWER ALL YOUR QUESTIONS!
THE WORLD OF NICK SZABO
AFTER LONG AND INTENSIVE DISCUSSIONS...
FASCINATING, YOUR FRIEND NICK!
WELL, STILL UNCLEAR! I DON'T UNDERSTAND HOW I CAN CONNECT YOUR DIGITAL WITH MY REAL WORLD! WHAT DO YOU THINK, EVA?
HUHM...
WHAT DO YOU MEAN?
NOTHING – FORGET ABOUT IT

The reason it is so hard for so many humans to understand cryptoassets is because these assets are not for us. They are being built for the machines.

Anthony Pompliano, Founder of Morgan Creek Digital Assets

17. Beyond the Blockchain

The Bitcoin blockchain is generally regarded as the original blockchain and as the first implementation of the new distributed ledger technology, or DLT. As we have seen, the rigid Bitcoin blockchain 1.0 was followed by the programmable Ethereum variant, virtually the blockchain 2.0. The third generation of blockchains, in the form of IOTA and hashgraphs, is now on the springboard. Continuous development is taking place in the area of distributed ledger technologies, which began with Bitcoin at a very rudimentary level.

However, Bitcoin enthusiasts consider the idea of Bitcoin being technically outdated (i.e., analogous to Napster or Myspace but in the crypto world) to be inaccurate. There are reasons for its technological inefficiencies and constraints: Bitcoin is supposed to be a highly secure and, if possible, censorship-resistant basic layer of a new, modularly growing financial system.

As such, research and further development work have not come to a standstill in either the Bitcoin or the Ethereum community. Scaling solutions, above all, are being worked on zealously. On Bitcoin's side, the Lightning Network and Liquid are the two best-known approaches (more on this in chapter 19), while sharding, Plasma and Caspar stand out as particularly promising for Ethereum (more on this in chapter 20). As we will see, scaling networks seem to work best if not every participant—or network node—has all the information at all times to keep the network synchronized.

The third blockchain generation is not really a blockchain in the sense of how we have discussed it in this book so far. Projects that are based on directed acyclical graph (DAG) technology, such as IOTA, Nano and Byteball, are therefore also described as post-blockchain concepts.

DAGs function according to a "horizontal" scheme, while blockchains are based on a "vertical" structure. In a blockchain, miners create new blocks and these are added to the chain. But the "horizontal" method of DAGs allows transactions to be linked to other transactions so that there is no need to wait for confirmation of the next block or for all network participants to acknowledge the update. The DAG model does not have miners, blocks or a chain, meaning that the concept is no longer a "blockchain."

The structure of a DAG resembles a "confused" network of numerous transactions. This is why it is often referred to as a tangle—a term that occurs frequently, especially in connection with the IOTA project. Fundamentally, however, the tangle and blockchains have the same properties; they are distributed databases built on peer-to-peer networks. Therefore, the tangle is also a validation mechanism for decentralized consensus finding.

How the Tangle Works

The tangle is created by linking individual transactions in the network. But in contrast to the blockchains of Bitcoin and Ethereum, miners are not responsible for confirming transactions. Instead, this task is the responsibility of all active tangle users. By confirming newly added transactions in the tangle, the entire transaction history is indirectly confirmed. A user does not pay a fee for processing their own transactions, but they have to confirm other transactions as well.

An algorithm ensures that network participants do not merely confirm their own transactions. The reason for this is obvious: it is important to prevent the problem of "double-spending" (described in the first chapter). As in a blockchain, the tangle must also ensure that value units—such as the IOTA token in the case of IOTA—cannot be double-spent within the network.

The more participants in the network who process transactions, the more transactions are processed, and the faster the theoretical processing times for outstanding transactions. It is this concept that could enable the better scaling of DAG projects. What leads to transaction bottlenecks in a blockchain and slows down the network could make a tangle safer and faster.

The IOTA project was developed by a hardware startup working on a new trinary microprocessor called "Jinn." In the future, this component could make it possible for every vehicle, every device and every appliance to communicate with each other via the IOTA network. Right from the start, the

IOTA project has been dedicated to the internet of things (IoT). Due to its potential scalability, it sees itself as the prospective solution for providing efficient transaction processing in a future machine-to-machine economy.

It already seems clear today that our world is developing in this direction. It is estimated that by 2025 there will be over 100 billion interconnected devices and machines worldwide, each with a dozen or more sensors. IOTA wants to function as a public, non-centralized and self-regulating machine-to-machine network through which machines can communicate and exchange value. This can be illustrated by an example of the smart car. This intelligent vehicle could one day have an identity and an e-wallet—an electronic purse. Thanks to this equipment, the car would be able to pay for fuel, insurance, cleaning or road tolls itself. Cryptocurrencies make it possible for each device to have its own bank account on the internet.

This future vehicle would not only be self-driving and be able to pay for services independently—it would also be able to sell its own services. Whenever a vehicle owner does not need their own vehicle, the vehicle would be able to offer its own driving services. The customer pays for the journey with their e-wallet. In this way, the car could generate a type of passive income for the owner instead of standing uselessly in a parking lot. If a passenger is in a hurry, they could also have the vehicle ask other vehicles to allow it to pass them and arrive first—for a fee, of course, which is paid directly to the other vehicles using a cryptocurrency.

The world's first electric vehicle charging station using IOTA payments went into operation in mid-April 2018 in the Netherlands. For the IOTA team, this is an important milestone on the road to the future and to real-world adoption. Ultimately, according to its founders, the IOTA network is to become the payment and settlement backbone as well as the data marketplace for all machines and equipment. This would create an economy of things in which data and values would merge and IoT devices would be able to share their digital assets autonomously.

In May 2018, the IOTA team revealed the Qubic protocol, which will be built on top of the IOTA tangle to support distributed computing as well as smart contracts and oracles providing data (more on this in chapter 15). In the long term, Qubic is intended to allow people on a global scale to take advantage of unused computing power for all kinds of computational needs, while helping to secure the IOTA tangle and enhance the performance of the network. Microtransactions should ensure that this unused external and distributed computer capacity can be used for the IOTA tangle.

The Future Vision of Hashgraph

Alongside the tangle, hashgraph is another concept, which is not based on blocks that are chronologically linked to form a chain, but on so-called "events" that are connected to each other, or hashed, technically speaking—hence the name hashgraph. In a blockchain, a new transaction is added to a specific chain, but in a hashgraph, all nodes within the network inform and "exchange" information with each other regarding the latest status of the network. Similar to the tangle, a connection diagram of chronologically ordered events or transactions is created.

A communication protocol called the gossip protocol distributes the information within the network. It is considered the fastest and most efficient method for exchanging data between computers. Each computer passes on the received information to a randomly selected computer, and so the information spreads across the network like wildfire.

However, this is not enough to achieve a general consensus about the shared data. In order for this to happen, each node must know the exact transaction history and therefore the specific sequence of the individual transactions. Time stamps ensure this. The hashgraph consensus algorithm uses the "gossip about gossip" approach in which each computer within the network shares all it knows regarding which node said what, to whom and when. Or to put it technically: through the hashgraph, each node shares its knowledge of the exact order of all transactions ever made on the network and the origins of that information.

Interestingly, some of the algorithms used in hashgraph technology are over 35 years old and are being applied here in a somewhat modified form. Hashgraph rates among the top in distributed ledger technology with regard to security as well. As long as less than a third of the users have no deliberate intentions of fraud, the connected computers should always find a consensus on the state and transaction history of the network, according to hashgraph proponents.

As such, the hashgraph algorithm is another application of distributed ledger technology. Just like blockchains, it is intended to change the structure and organization of today's internet in a radical way. As we have seen in chapter 14, today's World Wide Web has some serious weaknesses. Currently, its cornerstones are large centralized server facilities that offer plenty of opportunities for all kinds of attacks—hacks, spam, and botnet or DDoS attacks are part of everyday reality online.

The internet, which seems to connect everything, also suffers from isolation. It consists of separate systems, and smooth communication between them is complex and resource-intensive. Enthusiasts see hashgraph as a possible solution to these problems, that it could create an "internet of shared worlds" that minimizes the security risks and gaps, while eliminating isolation at the same time. And unlike conventional blockchains, hashgraph is designed to allow for scaling on its basic protocol.

Furthermore, the hashgraph protocol is intended to essentially change the model of internet data storage. Data should be better distributed within and across networks. As in the case of the IOTA network, hashgraph technology would allow users to be remunerated via micropayments for supplying their surplus data storage capacities. Expensive, centralized servers for data storage would then be eliminated, argue Hashgraph proponents.

In addition, hashgraph technology would make the internet faster than the current "leadership-based" network, which is built on central servers and has to route all data traffic through the system as a whole. For example, tests carried out with private hashgraph networks have resulted in higher transaction speeds than currently demonstrated by the Visa credit card network.

The hashgraph algorithm was developed in mid-2016 by Leemon Baird, the co-founder and CTO of Swirlds, which owns the hashgraph intellectual property rights. Swirlds distributes a software development program that allows anyone to experiment with hashgraph technology. They have already found a strong customer in CULedger, a consortium of 6,000 credit unions in North America, to use the hashgraph software.

Based on the initial successes in the corporate sector, Swirlds has launched the Hedera Hashgraph platform, which is intended to advance the development of a public hashgraph network. On September 16, 2019, the distributed ledger platform was launched as a public beta. It comprises three services: 1) a native coin by the acronym of HBAR, 2) smart contract capabilities to build applications and 3) a file service that lets external data be anchored to Hedera's public ledger—this way, external documents of any kind can be timestamped, which proves they existed at a certain point in time.

Hedera's native cryptocurrency is supposed to have two use cases related to its other two services: whoever wants to program a smart contract or anchor external data to Hashgraph's distributed ledger will have to pay transaction fees. These network fees will go to the nodes that uphold Hedera's ledger by providing bandwidth, computational power and storage. Aside from this, the HBAR token will also be used to secure Hedera's proof-of-stake consensus mechanism (more on proof of stake in chapter 21).

Although the source code of Hedera Hashgraph is publicly available and anyone can become part of the network as a node, the project has a governance model similar to that of Visa. Its governing council is initially comprised of 39 organizations and enterprises with equal voting power; this structure ensures that forks (i.e., splitting off the source code in order to create alternative projects) are not possible. Right now enterprises from across different industries are part of this governing council, such as Deutsche Telekom, IBM, Boeing or Swisscom Blockchain. At scale, thousands of public nodes are expected to join the network's decentralized consensus, according to the people behind hashgraph.

Great Expectations

Innovative approaches like tangle and hashgraph open a new chapter in the still-young history of distributed ledger technology, with mutual competition further boosting its innovative capacity. But there are also justified objections. In principle, the applications of DAG technology are based on regional consensus. Users do not store all transactions but only "local" data of their "neighbors" and trust that other "regions" will do so just as carefully. Critics argue that this concept of regionality cannot always prevent double-spend attacks.

There are also worries that centralization may occur among the tangle and hashgraph nodes that keep the networks running if the networks one day reach a huge data size due to their scalability. For example, IOTA has provided coordinators who would regularly shorten the tangle. But this would again give the network central points of attack. Also, Hedera Hashgraph does not seem to be a paradigm shift as the project is really just trading off validation for throughput. In reality, Hedera's 10,000 transactions per second—which only applies to its cryptocurrency, HBAR, and not its smart contract functionality—stem from the fact that its public ledger trades off a node's ability to validate the system in order to run a smaller network with greater speed. And even the so-called "state proofs" Hedera plans on enabling later will be centrally approved by Hedera itself, which doesn't solve anything.

So while Hedera actually plans on implementing centrality down the road, those responsible for IOTA argue that their coordinators merely fulfill a supporting role. Once the project reaches a certain size and relevance, the "training wheels" would no longer be necessary. At the end of May 2019, IOTA announced the Coordicide initiative, which aims to remove coordinators and speed up the network without sacrificing non-centrality. It proposes a new voting mechanism whereby one node seeks the opinion of other nodes to decide which transactions to include in the tangle and which to orphan. Due to its complexity, Coordicide is introduced modularly (i.e., component by component).

Although tangle and hashgraph are yet another attempt at achieving a distributed ledger, they have not yet provided practical proof of true decentralization. But this is by no means an argument against them. After all, it is the essence of the crypto world to try something new, fail and do it again—better. Or, as Bitcoiners affirm, one comes to realize that the correct path has already been taken right from the beginning.

FAST MONEY
ICO
I'LL BEAT YOU WITH YOUR OWN WEAPONS!
HEY KALI! HERBERT STARTED HIS OWN ICO! LET'S HAVE A CLOSER LOOK.
YOU'RE KIDDING?
"THE BEST ICO PROJECT EVER?"
PARTY TIME! BUY OUR COINS! YEAH!!!
AIR DROP PARTY!!!
WHITE PAPER
THIS IS DEFINITELY A SCAM!
KALI! WE NEED TO WARN THE PEOPLE!!!
HAHA... TOO LATE! YOU FELL FOR IT, BUNCH OF LOOOOSER!

Technology at its best: Bitcoin!

Arthur Vayloyan, CEO Bitcoin Suisse

18. Childhood Diseases of a New Technology

There seems to be hardly a life or area of business that has not been turned upside down by blockchain technology—at least in theory. In practice, however, things have been different so far.

Unlike Google, Facebook and Visa, public, permissionless blockchain networks such as Bitcoin and Ethereum are not yet widely used. Bitcoin is not a generally accepted means of payment nor does Ethereum's decentralized world computer serve as a basis for everyday applications. Their definitive flaw: compared to traditional systems, Bitcoin and Ethereum are still far too slow.

The payment service PayPal, for example, processes around 200 transactions per second, while the credit card provider Visa processes as many as 56,000. Platforms such as Google and Facebook process even more data all at once, playing in a different league altogether. Ethereum, on the other hand, manages an average of 20 transactions per second, while Bitcoin is capable of handling between 3 and 10 transactions a second.

There is a reason why blockchain systems currently cannot even come close to the transaction capacities of the dominant legacy systems: the so-called blockchain trilemma. At present, a public, permissionless blockchain can fulfill simultaneously only the first two of the following three properties: non-centrality, security and scalability.

Applications such as Google and Facebook are able to achieve high transaction capacity only because they prioritize scalability and security and almost completely neglect decentralization. In contrast, choosing a public blockchain means prioritizing non-centrality and security over scalability.

The Bitcoin blockchain, for example, allows anyone who wants to operate a network-bearing node, also known as a full node, to do so without reservation. Because each full node processes and records each individual transaction, it has the entire transaction history of the blockchain at its disposal, ensuring that the entire system is kept synchronized.

Full nodes are important pillars of the Bitcoin network. They are convinced that they can verify all transactions and make this information available to other users free of charge. Because they are the only network participants with the complete transaction history, they can always verify that no bitcoin are issued twice. Full nodes are highly regarded in the community because without them the blockchain would not be stored anywhere.

But a network built in this way is only as strong as its weakest link, which is why scalability and thus transaction capacity and speed depend to some extent on the computing capacity of the weakest nodes. These network nodes could, of course, be discarded to make the system faster. But then the blockchain would have disregarded its goal of being as public and permissionless as possible.

Unresolved Scaling Problems

The Bitcoin community has always discussed how best to scale Bitcoin—a search that culminated in the so-called block size debate. As we saw at the beginning of this book, the Bitcoin system consists of blocks that link together to form a chain, the blockchain. Like a container, a block combines individual transactions. Since each block has a limited data capacity, it can hold only a limited number of transactions. In Bitcoin, this block size has a bandwidth of 1 to 4 megabytes. The largest Bitcoin block to date was mined in October 2018, with a data capacity of around 2.3 megabytes.

But increasing the block size is not as easy as it might seem. Larger blocks require more data volume. As a result, the data volume of the blockchain increases overall. The larger the data volume of the blockchain, the more resource-intensive it becomes for the full nodes to continue downloading the entire blockchain for validation purposes. The demands on them would increase: the larger the blocks, the more computing power, memory, internet bandwidth and storage space a computer acting as a full node requires. Not everyone can cope with this, so some full nodes would have to give up.

When this scenario is thought out to the end, it's evident that block enlargement could lead to a situation in which only a few full nodes or even just one supercomputer might maintain the Bitcoin network at some point. This would jeopardize the two cornerstones of the Bitcoin network—decentralization and security—or make them altogether obsolete. Bitcoin would become more dependent on third parties and less trust-minimizing.

Because a part of the Bitcoin community did not want to take this risk under any circumstances, it vehemently opposed an expansion of the block size. But another faction saw it differently. As a consequence of the block size debate, Bitcoin Cash split off from Bitcoin as a hard fork on August 1, 2017. Bitcoin Cash's block size was increased to 8 megabytes, with the option of further expansion if necessary.

Whether it's blocks of 4, 10 or more megabytes, no one can know beforehand which block size might drive away too many full nodes and compromise the cornerstones of the system. In this sense, the spin-off of Bitcoin Cash is an offer to the market. Thanks to Bitcoin and Bitcoin Cash, investors can choose between similar but nevertheless fundamentally different assets—or reject both if neither is convincing. In any case, the debate about block size could not have provided concrete figures anyway. On the meta level, it revolved around a much more important question than 2 or 4 megabytes: Should Bitcoin primarily be a revolutionary counter-model to the classic world of finance, as the Bitcoin hard-liners have in mind? Or a global payment system that must be as scalable as possible in order to compete with Visa and the likes, as the Bitcoin pragmatists would have it?

Anyone with the former belief in mind must necessarily reject all changes that might lead Bitcoin to become in any way a real alternative and more similar to the current financial system, which is based heavily on human trust and technical scaling. But even the conservative decision to leave the block size unchanged (and thus accept that the network might never be scaled) does not guarantee that the data volume of the Bitcoin blockchain will not become too large anyway in a few decades—and therefore no longer be manageable for a full node even without a change. The dogmatists thus rely on technological progress in data storage and transmission so that computers can keep pace with the growth of data volumes.

From the point of view of the blockchain trilemma, the increase in block size acts as a measure in favor of scalability. In contrast, it does a disservice to non-centrality and thus security—and that cannot work out in the long run. From the hard-liners' point of view, new modular scaling approaches are needed in the near future to increase the capacity of the overall system without abandoning the fundamental properties of security and non-centrality.

Additional Protocols as a Solution

New possibilities of modular scaling have been raised by the famous Segregated Witness, or SegWit, update. This protocol update launched in August 2017, replacing Bitcoin's block size limit with a block weight limit. This means that with SegWit, transaction signature data is separated away from the transaction block and stored elsewhere (more on digital signatures in chapter 29), freeing up block capacity.

SegWit was originally initiated to fix transaction malleability, a flaw in the Bitcoin protocol that allowed transaction identities to be changed. As a nice side effect, however, it led to an increase in data throughput per block, allowing the Bitcoin network to process more transaction data. With the introduction of SegWit, the capacity of the individual Bitcoin blocks grew without changing their size. But even with SegWit, the capacity of the blocks is not infinite, and at some point the improved system will reach its limits.

What actually happens if the number of Bitcoin transactions exceeds the available capacities? Verified requests are sent to the queue, the so-called memory pool, or mempool. There, these transactions wait to be included in a future Bitcoin block. They are selected by the Bitcoin miners according to the transaction fee offered. Although a miner can choose any transaction, they will usually first process the one that earns them the most fees, and all other transactions must wait.

In December 2017, during the height of the hype when all the world seemed to have bought bitcoin, the fees that guaranteed the fastest possible execution were around $60 per transaction. Those who paid less were lucky if their transactions were processed and confirmed after hours or even days. The mempool was overloaded with more than 250,000 transactions waiting for confirmation. The Bitcoin network was stretched to its limits; part of the Bitcoin community had warned against such a fiasco years earlier.

The SegWit update allows for the development and implementation of second-layer protocols to prevent this from happening again. These are additional independent protocols built on top of the basic Bitcoin protocol that can relieve the load on the base-layer blockchain by processing transactions off-chain—while retaining the important properties of non-centrality and security. In this way, Bitcoin is to become scalable without the data traffic on the blockchain and the load on the full nodes having to increase. Read more about this in the next chapter.

HOUSTON, WE HAVE A PROBLEM
KALI, CHECK OUT THE BLOCKS. THEY'RE TOO SMALL AND SLOWING DOWN THE BLOCKCHAIN!
COMING THROUGH!
HAVE YOU EVER HEARD ABOUT THE LIGHTNING NETWORK?
QUICK AS A FLASH, SMALLER FEES AND EVEN MORE PRIVACY.
LIGHTNING ENABLES BITCOIN TO SCALE!
WITH THIS WE'LL EXPAND BITCOIN TO EVERYONE!
AFTER A TALK WITH THE EXPERTS...
SCALING WITH ADDITIONAL PROTOCOLS MAKES PERFECT SENSE!
WITH THIS, THE CRYPTO WORLD MAKES A QUANTUM LEAP FORWARD!
ONE MONTH LATER...
HEY JAY, I DON'T FULLY UNDERSTAND LIGHTNING NETWORK YET, BUT IT SAYS HERE THAT IT'S GROWING RAPIDLY!

Bitcoin and Lightning are tools in our repertoire, and like any other tool they are suitable for some applications but not for others.

Christian Decker, Lightning Expert Blockstream

19. Lightning Fast

As we discussed in the last chapter, the Bitcoin blockchain still works too slowly. The second-layer Lightning protocol is supposed to change that.

We can imagine Lightning as a superordinate network of off-chain payment channels. Two Lightning users can be part of such a channel, and at least one party must "fill it up" with bitcoin. If the parties have agreed to the establishment of a payment channel, it can be opened by initiating a transaction on the Bitcoin blockchain, which transfers the desired number of bitcoin units into the channel. Both participants can then execute any number of Bitcoin transactions with each other. After each transaction, the overall balance in the channel is updated so that the users can see who is entitled to how many bitcoin.

Either participant can choose to close the channel at any time by triggering a closing transaction on the Bitcoin blockchain. Each user receives the amount of bitcoin they are entitled to according to the final balance of the payment channel, and the bitcoin units are transferred on-chain again. The longer the channel remains open, the more profitable it is for those involved since they can avoid on-chain transaction fees on the Bitcoin blockchain.

Theoretically, payment channels can remain open indefinitely and serve any purpose. For example, a user can open a payment channel with their trusted coffee shop and pay for their cappuccino every morning using Lightning. To illustrate the Lightning Network in relation to the Bitcoin blockchain, the analogy of the gold standard (discussed in chapter 7) can be used again. In the past, gold was used to settle transactions. But since the precious metal is difficult to transport and expensive to store, paper certificates that could be exchanged for gold circulated for the sake of simplicity.

Lightning transactions resemble payment with certificates that represent ownership of bitcoin units. However, unlike most gold and money certificates issued by banks, Lightning promissory notes are fully secured and redeemable at all times. Thanks to cryptography, smart contracts and a sophisticated incentive structure, the protocol ensures that no Lightning user can cheat another. As mentioned, both parties must agree to the opening of a payment channel, but it can be closed one-sidedly. This is important, for example, if a party dies or is permanently disconnected from the internet and thus from the Lighting Network for other reasons. Then the bitcoin units remaining in the off-chain payment channel are not blocked or lost forever. This allows network participants to open payment channels with anonymous counterparties without taking any great risks.

Also, the parties cannot fool each other regarding the current balance within the payment channel. If one of the parties, who we will call Alice, refuses payment by closing the channel, all bitcoin are automatically frozen for a certain period of time as a security measure due to the unilateral termination. During this time, the other party, who we'll call Bob, can react. As a penalty to the fraudulent party, Lightning allows Bob to initiate a transaction that will transfer to him not only the bitcoin to which he is entitled, but all the bitcoin units in the payment channel. Bob must, however, prove that the unilateral channel closure triggered by Alice was not legal, for example, by presenting a more recent transaction status.

This punishment mechanism effectively discourages fraudsters. So far, attempts of fraud have hardly occurred on the Lightning network. But for this control and punishment system to work properly, Bob must continuously go online and connect to the Lightning Network to make sure he does not become a victim of a one-way payment channel closure. Currently, running a payment channel requires a lot of accounting and monitoring.

In the future, so-called "watchtowers" will populate the network and take over this task on behalf of Bob. Watchtowers are Lightning nodes whose services users can book. If such a guard detects a dishonest transaction by Alice in Bob's absence, it can trigger a punitive transaction in Bob's name. Bob will, in turn, compensate the watchtower by automatically remitting a pre-arranged fee. This way, people don't always have to be online in order for the Lightning Network to work smoothly. Critics argue that by hiring a watchtower Bob does rely on a trusted third party to read the blockchain on his behalf. To circumvent this, Bob would need to run his own Lightning full node.

From Channel to Network

So far, we've looked at a single payment channel. But Lightning is a network by name. This does not mean that a Lightning user has to open a payment channel with every other party in the network. Through a process called routing, a payment can be sent to any recipient via several users. Computer science also refers to the "leaps" from one user to another as "hops." In this way, Alice can send bitcoin units via Bob to Carol without opening her own payment channel with Carol.

Here, too, cryptography and incentive structures guarantee that the routing points between the sender and recipient are not fraudulent and that the bitcoin units cannot be pocketed illegally. The routing in Lightning is designed in such a way that human trust is not necessary. So Alice doesn't have to trust Bob but can still be sure that her bitcoin will be received by Carol in a secure way.

Over time, because of this routing structure, nodes that have open payment channels with many users are likely to establish themselves within the network and therefore handle a significant portion of the Lightning payment traffic. In this respect, these payment hubs are not dissimilar to today's banks; similarly, these nodes are likely to charge fees for their services sooner or later. However, they are unlikely to turn into bottlenecks that users necessarily have to go through, because the market is highly competitive and it is also possible to circumvent these hubs by clever routing.

Nevertheless, this potential development somewhat dampens the hope that the Lightning Network can be used completely free of charge. And the fact that Lightning is pushing the development of a kind of banking system on the Bitcoin blockchain is viewed with great skepticism by some Bitcoiners. Even if cryptographic methods guarantee that Lightning is less dependent on trust than the conventional banking system, large routing service providers are likely to dominate the network one day. And it is only a matter of time before a loan-and-credit economy with interest and savings also emerges on the protocol with base layer bitcoin serving as the so-called risk-free asset.

Once again, the trilemma discussed in the last chapter shows that scaling the Bitcoin system is at the expense of non-centrality and thus security and censorship resistance. In contrast to the traditional financial system, however, centralization can be outsourced to the second-layer Lightning protocol. The Bitcoin basic layer remains non-central and secure, and ensures, for example, that no uncovered bitcoin claims circulate in Lightning, as is the case in the traditional financial world (see chapter 5). The basic protocol thus has a securing and, at the same time, moderating effect on the additional protocols.

Rising Transaction Costs

Midway through 2019, Lightning is still in its infancy. Full participation (i.e., sending and receiving Bitcoin payments) is possible only if you operate a fully fledged Lightning node. Not all people have the necessary technical expertise.

In addition, routing does not yet work properly. For example, if Alice wants to transfer 4 bitcoin to Dave and has to go through Bob and Carol because she and Dave do not have a direct payment channel, Bob and Carol must also have at least 4 bitcoin in their payment channels.

Larger remittances are currently likely to fail because of this condition, but Atomic Multi-Path Payments (AMPs) are expected to solve this problem soon. A large payment is split into many small payments and routed via various hops. This splicing should simplify the use of Lightning: a user could load or unload any existing payment channel with just one on-chain transaction on the Bitcoin base layer. By splicing out for example, one can close a channel, pay on-chain and open a new channel in one single on-chain transaction.

For users not to have to freeze a separate amount of bitcoin for each of their payment channels, developers are currently working on a concept called channel factories. These are a type of payment hub that contains many users, and gives a user access to many payment channels, which should also help to keep the Lighting Network non-central.

Another issue is that Lightning user interfaces are currently not very intuitive. But this area should also improve steadily, not unlike the bulky-looking web browsers, email programs and streaming platforms of the past. In the long run, users will likely have access to applications that run seamlessly on the Lightning Network.

Though the add-on Lightning protocol currently appears to be Bitcoin's most promising scaling attempt, critical voices are of course not missing here either. Some people point out that Lightning scales the number of transactions but not the number of users. Others complain that on-chain transactions still have to take place to use the additional protocol.

On-chain transactions are likely to become more and more expensive because the block reward for miners (more on this in chapters 1 and 3) decreases every four years, and without higher fees their incentive to mine new

Bitcoin blocks would decrease. Higher on-chain transaction fees, however, make it more difficult to open up Lightning payment channels that are free in themselves.

The rising fees also increase access barriers to the Bitcoin world, which limits their social scalability (more on this in chapter 2). Similar to today's banking system, many and more people could be indirectly excluded from the network because they simply cannot afford to participate. If this were to happen, Bitcoin would have to put up with the accusation of being new wine in old bottles.

This is why Bitcoin Cash proponents are skeptical of the Lightning Network and would rather focus on on-chain scaling. As we have seen in chapter 18, this would cause greater centralization of the network, much to the detriment of running a full node. Does this mean that Bitcoin Cash does not serve any purpose at all? But seeing it this way might just be jumping the gun.

To Bitcoiners, Bitcoin Cash might seem centralized on the full-node side, which is why they often refer to it as PayPal 2.0. But this is not quite accurate since Bitcoin Cash offers way cheaper payments to its users. In a sense, Bitcoin's biggest fork would rather be called "PayPal for the poor." In comparison to the famous payment processor, Bitcoin Cash allows for money transactions at a fraction of PayPal's costs and needs much fewer touchpoints with traditional finance. Most definitely an improvement.

Liquid and Other Sidechains

Lightning is by no means the only additional protocol launched on the Bitcoin base layer. Sidechains are independent blockchains with their own rules that are connected to the Bitcoin blockchain, which is usually referred to as the mainchain. Basically, sidechains make possible what the Bitcoin blockchain cannot do. For example, the sidechain Mimblewimble provides privacy, while Turing completeness and thus complex smart-contract functionalities can be found with the Rootstock sidechain. And those who want to tokenize assets with Bitcoin inevitably end up using Liquid.

The Liquid sidechain, launched at the end of 2018, uses the Liquid bitcoin (L-BTC) token as its own currency, which is coupled to bitcoin—this guarantees a fixed exchange rate between the two assets. To issue Liquid bitcoin, bitcoin units must be transferred from the mainchain to the sidechain. During the time they are on the sidechain, they are frozen on the base-layer blockchain. If the user moves the bitcoin back, the corresponding Liquid bitcoin units are deleted, and the mainchain releases the locked bitcoin. In order to transfer bitcoin from the sidechain back to the mainchain, the Liquid user must go through so-called Liquid functionaries, which are somewhat comparable to Bitcoin miners. The sidechain functions according to different rules than the Bitcoin blockchain—and pursues different goals. The creation of a new block with Liquid does not take ten minutes as with the Bitcoin mainchain, but only two. A transaction is therefore completed much faster. This is also because the payments are authorized and not mined. Sidechain transactions, like Lightning transactions, are confidential and visible only to Liquid functionaries, giving users more privacy than on the Bitcoin mainchain.

Of course, sidechains cannot simply make away with the Blockchain trilemma. In the case of Liquid, the priorities are—once again—shifted from non-centrality to scaling. Thus the Liquid sidechain is most similar to a "federated blockchain" (more about this in chapter 9).

Liquid is open source, can be validated by individual users and is accessible to all interested parties. The functionaries who form the network, however, are active as administrative authorities on the Liquid network. They handle the changes from the mainchain to the sidechain and back. They also authorize new blocks on the Liquid blockchain, and as nodes, they validate all network transactions.

The functionaries cannot change the Liquid blockchain, but they have the option not to execute required bitcoin transfers from the sidechain to the mainchain. In a sense, they control the use of the assets. At worst, they can even steal them if they conspire against Liquid users. This is a fact that anyone wanting to take advantage of Liquid must be aware of.

The protocol can be used to tokenize all kinds of assets through the Bitcoin system, including government fiat currencies, digital collectibles, certified assets, and utility or security tokens (see chapter 12 for more). Even the tokenization of alternative cryptoassets, also known as alternative coins or altcoins, can be done via the Liquid blockchain, which in turn facilitates atomic swaps (i.e., token trading across different blockchains).

In theory, Bitcoin sidechains such as Liquid could even make altcoins obsolete because they make possible what the different altcoins strive for—but on the solid basis of the non-central and trust-minimizing Bitcoin.

RESEARCH AT THE ACADEMY
BASEL, SWITZERLAND
WELCOME TO THE FIRST FACULTY IN BLOCKCHAIN, EVER! I'LL SHOW YOU AROUND!
OUR DEGREES ARE BEING STORED ON BLOCKCHAIN.
IT ENSURES THAT NONE OF THEM CAN BE FALSIFIED!
THAT'S UNIQUE!
WE FOCUS ON THE CRYPTO ECONOMY, A BRAND NEW INTERDISCIPLINARY TOPIC!
AND WORK ON A COMPLETELY NEW WORLD OF CRYPTO ASSETS!
THIS IS OUR "GODZILLA", A TOKENIZATION MACHINE!

Blockchain is successful
when people don't know they are using it.

Johannes Schweifer, CEO CoreLedger

20. Conflict of Visions

After the crash of the bitcoin price and the arrival of crypto winter in 2018, Ethereum, the world's number-two cryptoasset, was badly hit as well. Since the cryptocurrency had positioned itself not only as sound money for the 21st century, but also as a world computer, the criticism about its lack of success was all the harsher. The countless promises of a soon-flourishing web 3.0 had hardly been fulfilled, and disillusionment was huge.

The biggest problem here was scaling. As with Bitcoin, Ethereum's "simple" scaling paths do not lead to the envisioned goals—neither an increase of the block size limit nor the implementation of individual blockchains independent of each other. The community also rejected the possibility of merge mining, which would have allowed different blockchains to benefit from the same mining power. Through merge mining, it might be possible to increase transaction throughput without compromising the security of the blockchain, though this point is questioned. The concerns that merge mining would increase the demands on individual miners, which would increasingly centralize mining, also weigh heavily.

Both Bitcoin and Ethereum agree on this one aspect: the blockchain trilemma should be solved without each node having to become a supercomputer and requiring several terabytes of storage capacity. Saving, processing, downloading and re-feeding transactions into the network should therefore be distributed over several layers.

We've already learned about these second-layer scaling solutions, having discussed the example of the Lightning Network in the previous chapter. They should enable transactions off-chain (i.e., outside the main blockchain, also called the main chain), and if implemented correctly, second-layer solutions should indirectly scale a blockchain without having to cut back on non-centrality and security. One possibility of off-chain scaling with Ethereum is state channels, which work in a similar way to Lightning payment channels on Bitcoin. To open a state channel, users trigger the corresponding transaction on the Ethereum blockchain. Then, once open, an infinite number of transactions can theoretically be carried out off-chain—just like on the Lightning Network. A second blockchain transaction closes the state channel again. Then the relevant state (i.e., the balance of the channel based on the off-chain transactions) is communicated to the base-layer blockchain and anchored there as the new state.

Sidechains, or child chains, are another promising second-layer scaling attempt. Within Bitcoin, they are currently applicable in the form of Liquid and a few other protocols (more on this in chapter 19). On the Ethereum blockchain, the comparable framework is called Plasma. Childchains are pegged to the base-layer blockchain, and they are in constant communication, ensuring that all transactions are booked correctly.

One of the biggest challenges for second-layer implementations such as Plasma is the communication link between the child chain and the main chain: it should be designed to minimize trust as much as possible. Developers are currently pursuing several different approaches to find the most effective solution.

The Big Plan

The scaling of Ethereum will lead to a strong change in its public blockchain in the coming years. Ethereum 2.0 will replace the current blockchain and further versions will follow in the future.

An update called "Serenity" is supposed to initiate the transition to Ethereum 2.0. This will change the consensus algorithm from proof of work (PoW) to proof of stake (PoS), and miners will be replaced by stakers. Fully merging the old Ethereum PoW chain into the new PoS network will most likely take years. So far consensus is that transfer of ether between the two chains will not be possible because the security risk of messing either chain and with it Ethereum 1.0 as well as Ethereum 2.0 is too great. However, there are some first proposals on how to enable transfers through secure methods.

Let's suppose everything works out fine, then by the time the transition is done, Ethereum will no longer need external power to create new blocks, but will try to achieve a constant consensus through game theory alone (more about this in chapter 21). In the first phase of the transition, a new blockchain called the beacon chain will be implemented to run in parallel with today's proof-of-work chain. The beacon chain is a central building block of Ethereum 2.0. As we will see later, it will be the PoS network's heartbeat and coordinate activity across the network.

Another approach to scaling Ethereum's basic blockchain is sharding, which was briefly mentioned in chapter 17. A public blockchain like Ethereum contains all relevant information about past transactions. A kind of gossip protocol ensures that all nodes in the system share all information with the other nodes. Because of this complete transaction history, nodes cannot deceive others. Since everyone knows everything, there is complete transparency.

But it is precisely this feature that makes the system very inefficient in terms of speed and throughput. The network can process transactions only as fast as its individual nodes can, and not as fast as the sum of all nodes (i.e., the world computer) would allow.

The concept of sharding would help here, in which the entire state of the Ethereum network is split into small independent parts, or so-called shards. The respective shards have their own state—they are small sub-blockchains each with their own transaction history, and together they make up the Ethereum blockchain.

Each individual shard has a committee of 128 validators that process and verify a certain number of transactions. An Ethereum blockchain based on sharding should be able to process multiple transactions in parallel. In its first phase, the Serenity update is planned to implement 1,024 shards, according to mid-2019 figures. However, the number of shards is changeable since sharding is dynamic and can be adapted to various circumstances. It is the visionary behind Ethereum, Vitalik Buterin, that has proposed to cut the number of shards down to 64. This way, communication between shards would be faster an simpler. With this number of shards, the transaction capacity of Ethereum 2.0 would also be lower though.

Still, sharding is regarded as one of the most promising attempts to significantly scale public blockchains, but some problems have yet to be solved. On the one hand, the independent shards must be able to come together again to form a unity. On the other hand, flawless communication between the individual shards, or the "cross-shard communication," must be ensured.

The beacon chain mentioned earlier is intended to solve the first problem. Its task is to sum up the blocks produced by the individual shards into a global, all-encompassing state for the entire Ethereum network. Only when the state of a shard corresponds cryptographically with the corresponding hashes of the base-layer blockchain (the beacon chain) are the transactions within the shard considered verified. The beacon chain can be viewed as a sort of command center aggregating data about confirmed transactions for all shards.

The nodes in the beacon chain must meet higher hardware requirements than simple users in terms of computing power, memory and internet bandwidth. Each of these beacon nodes is directly connected to the validators of the shards to keep both chains synchronized. Due to the higher requirements, a potential increase in centralization is more likely with beacon nodes.

Meanwhile, shards are vulnerable to attacks because "smaller" blockchains require a much smaller critical mass for a successful attack. Randomization, which takes place at the beacon chain level, is intended to counteract this. After 64 newly created blocks, or about 6.4 minutes, the validators are shuffled and assigned to new shards.

In this way, a constant mixing of the validating committees takes place, which in turn increases the security of each individual shard. Rotating the validators lessens the likelihood that the malicious ones among them could gather together. However, if individual validators randomly gain control over a shard, they will only be able to exercise it for a total of 64 blocks or about 6.4 minutes.

At the beginning of 2018, developers presented a total of six proposed solutions to improve cross-shard communication. None of them are perfect, due to various time, cost or implementation reasons; all have their inefficiencies in one or the other way. And the reason for this is sharding itself.

Its main purpose is to divide the Ethereum blockchain into independent sub-blockchains that don't need to know anything about each other to work. At the same time, they need to form Ethereum 2.0 together as a whole—and thus know about each other again, especially if individual transactions are processed over several shards. Ethereum's long-term success depends on the resolution of this dilemma.

Battle of the Giants

Like Bitcoin before it, Ethereum has captivated many people. Software developers in particular could take their first steps into the crypto world thanks to the existence of the programmable blockchain. But the fact that Ethereum was created as a further development from the less flexible Bitcoin blockchain has caused tension between the two leading cryptoassets right from the start.

Over time, the rivalry between the two camps seems to have increased. Some Bitcoin enthusiasts see Ethereum as just a cheap copy of Bitcoin, which would hardly be faithful to the philosophy of the crypto world. On the Ethereum side, some exponents say that their programmable blockchain is far superior to that of Bitcoin and that it will make it obsolete sooner rather than later.

The reason these two crypto communities are at loggerheads with each other is probably due to the fact that they view the world fundamentally differently—for which the U.S. economist Thomas Sowell coined the term "conflict of visions." He distinguishes between constrained and unconstrained visions.

The constrained vision assumes that certain realities—such as the scarcity of natural resources or human egoism—are given and unchangeable. According to this view, human irrationality, for example, can never be completely eradicated by technology. It is therefore necessary to understand the laws of nature and the limits of humankind and to promote innovation within these parameters.

In the constrained vision, all solutions are trade-offs, because the goals set are partly diametrically opposed to each other and therefore compromises are necessary. As a result, none of the goals are completely achieved and some needs always remain unfulfilled.

The unconstrained vision, as the name implies, does not accept limitations, neither natural nor human. There are no limits to imagination. In order to achieve goals and solve problems, the unconstrained vision aims to shape the world and people as it pleases. It strives for the perfect solution, without or with only a few compromises.

The vision of the Bitcoin project is constrained; the community pursues a conservative strategy. Network non-centralization, security and reliability are top priorities, while the scaling goal is subordinate to the first three. Bitcoin supporters are convinced that the development of the cryptocurrency is subject to fundamental trade-offs and that progress is always gradual. The functionality of the blockchain is their first priority. In order to guarantee it at all times, they are prepared to make all kinds of compromises. The Ethereum community, on the other hand, seems to be mostly in line with the unconstrained vision in its thinking and actions. Ethereum was created from the beginning with an "unlimited software development" mentality. "Be quick, break things" is a slogan that Ethereum enthusiasts often utter. In their view, technological innovation is the highest goal, and possible problems can always be defused after the fact. Of course, the Ethereum community also takes safety seriously and makes compromises. The latter, however, is much rarer than with Bitcoiners.

The fact that people feel attracted to different projects is neither surprising nor reprehensible. As we know from elections, everyone chooses the side they think is more in line with their own attitude and viewpoints. It is therefore not clear whether Bitcoin and Ethereum are actually involved in a predatory competition or whether they simply satisfy different needs, being apex predators in their respective fields, with well-established, loyal followings.

For the sake of greater experimentation and flexibility in the programmability of the blockchain, the Ethereum community accepts a greater susceptibility to errors. This is reflected in events like the DAO hack, the Parity bug and other setbacks that were due to programming errors.

Initial design decisions have made Bitcoin a global, robust, secure and censorship-resistant store of value. The Bitcoin blockchain currently offers the highest level of security of any crypto system. This implies, however, that Bitcoin is necessarily based on a rudimentary script that is difficult to program. On the other hand, the vulnerability to bugs is comparatively low.

Bitcoin uses a modular scaling method that builds layer by layer and keeps the individual layers as simple as possible. As in the case of the Linux operating system, the community relies on modular and simply built systems being more flexible, more robust and more versatile than Microsoft's Windows operating system, for example, which has always come across as a more-or-less fixed stack.

These modular systems rely on "Gall's Law," established by the American system theorist John Gall: "A complex system that works is invariably found to have evolved from a simple system that worked. A complex system designed from scratch never works and cannot be patched up to make it work. You have to start over, beginning with a working simple system."

A certain modularity in the scaling of Ethereum cannot be denied either. Nonetheless, Gall's words might not be taken so well by the community of the second-largest cryptoasset. But they have web 3.0 in mind, after all, and must therefore equip the basic layer with greater complexity—if they want to succeed at all. But even the inventor of Ethereum, Vitalik Buterin, realizes that infinite complexity in relation to the base layer is not desirable. Thus, in the long run, the developers should agree on a definitive base layer, which could then potentially ossify and remain unchanged for all eternity. Of course, the Ethereum community is positive that this undertaking will succeed, while Bitcoin supporters remain more skeptical.

Quest for the Better Money

Some—most famously the blockchain expert and advocate Andreas Antonopoulos—have stated that Bitcoin and Ethereum are not really fighting the same battle. Bitcoin is a lion and Ethereum is a shark. Both are apex predators in their respective environments. But it might turn out that the two are fighting in the same quest for a better form of programmable money after all.

In their mission to conquer and alter today's financial system, two broadly different visions can be extracted. Bitcoin is being touted as a new base-layer-settlement money to disrupt central banks, but not necessarily commercial banks. Meanwhile, Ethereum is really after private banks, eager to replace them with code, with the belief that eventually, saving, lending, borrowing and trading should be done through protocols—completely bankless (more on this in chapter 16).

Which of these visions will ultimately be realized depends very much on how the two cryptoassets perform as true and functioning money. Whether this will happen is again dependent on the mandate of cryptoasset monetary policy, which is: to maximally secure the network at minimum cost. In the case of Bitcoin and Ethereum, it would probably make more sense to compare their issuance and even security policies.

For both Bitcoin and Ethereum, the security of the network is built on economic incentives related to their corresponding consensus mechanisms (more on this in chapter 20). To date, both networks rely on miners to provide capital in the form of hardware and energy to uphold the network. The compensation miners receive comes from two sources: block rewards (newly minted bitcoin or ether) and transaction fees earned from users (i.e., spenders in the network). The total sum of both—block rewards and transaction fees—is miner revenue. And miner revenue is essentially equal to security budget.

In Bitcoin, block rewards are cut in half about once every four years (referred to as the "halvening"), asymptotically approaching zero. Reducing block rewards reinforces Bitcoin's narrative of absolute scarcity (more on this in chapter 3). At the same time, the security subsidy is cut as well with every halvening. Currently, the maintenance of the Bitcoin network costs miners about $5 billion USD a year, and around 95 percent of that cost is covered by block rewards (i.e., inflation). Bitcoin is deriving its security from the value of bitcoin itself. In order for this to be the case in the future, the value of bitcoin has to rise in tandem with the cost of maintaining the network. Alternatively, the security budget would have to come from a secondary market of fees for block space.

There is absolutely no deterministic reason why the cryptoasset's value should not be able to keep up with the cost of network maintenance. And it is just as possible that in the future, there will be enough users of block space (or simply referred to as spenders) to generate enough revenue for miners to uphold the network. But there's also the chance that the market will find bitcoin useful for holding, which will translate to low transaction fees. Because of the cryptoasset's absolute scarcity, this scenario is one that is quite likely. And herein lies the crux of the matter: Bitcoin is designed to reward the saver but will ironically be ever more dependent on the spender—the saver's counterpart. Once inflation is gone and 100 percent of miners' revenues come from transaction fees, spenders will generate a positive externality for the savers, who will benefit from the existence of the network but will not have to pay anything annually for the network to exist. Can such a network exist, which completely favors one group over another?

The community behind Ethereum would say no, which is why this crypto network's monetary/security policy is one of minimum necessary issuance. This means that the issuance of block rewards is only as high as is needed to achieve maximum security of the Ethereum network at minimal cost. This certainly has the trade-off that Ethereum's scarcity narrative is nowhere as strong as Bitcoin's. But then again, because Ethereum is funding security with block rewards, its security budget will never be 100 percent reliant on transaction fees. If you ask Ethereum proponents, they will simply tell you: This is as good as we can get. Sounds like a constrained vision after all…

NEVER GIVE UP!
THE PRICES OF CRYPTOCURRENCIES HAVE PLUMMETED BY HALF TODAY! PANIC AT THE MARKET...
LORD IB VON KRATZ, DID YOU SEE THIS COMING?
I ALWAYS SAID BITCOIN IS A TICKING TIME BOMB!
MANY INVESTORS HAVE LOST MONEY! IF ONLY THEY HAD LISTENED TO ME.
...BITCOIN WILL DISAPPEAR AND IN A FEW YEARS IT'LL BE BUT A FAINT MEMORY.
WHAT A HOGWASH! THIS IS JUST A TEMPORARY CORRECTION. THE PRICE WILL RECOVER!
BITCOIN HAS WITHSTOOD MANY BATTLE AND IS SO TO SPEAK - ANTIFRAGILE!
YEAH, NO WONDER - CHECK OUT THE CROWD ON THE STREET. THEY'RE FIGHTING AGAINST THESE PANIC MAKERS.
IN ADDITION, BITCOIN FOLLOWS A FRACTAL PRICE PATTERN.
WITH EVERY HALVENING, THE WAVE PEAKS EVEN MORE!
WE BELIEVE IN BITCOIN!
HODL!

Proof-of-stake is a political system
where the voters get paid by the non-voters.

Tuur Demeester, Founder Adamant Capital

21. Disagreeing on Consensus

The Bitcoin blockchain functions seamlessly due to its cleverly balanced incentive structure. It is based on a proof-of-work (PoW) mechanism, which the system uses to find consensus, allowing every user to check which transactions have been carried out in which order. This means that there is always consensus about who owns what and when in the network (more on this in chapter 9). However, what sounds simple is extremely complicated in practice.

As we already know, the Bitcoin blockchain is a radically non-central system that avoids relying on authorities from outside. One of these areas inevitably involves the measurement of time. Every clock we know depends on a third party—for example, an internet provider, the operator of a mobile phone network or a church that owns a clock tower. These are central anchor points on which Bitcoin does not want to rely. However, it is not so easy to ensure a chronological sequence of transactions without referring to an absolute time set by the outside world.

Something as self-evident as time suddenly becomes a problem in a non-central network. Without a consistent way to measure time, there is no consistent way to distinguish before and after.

With the implementation of proof of work, the anonymous inventor of Bitcoin, Satoshi Nakamoto, solved this problem by creating a probabilistic non-central "clock." While mining (more on this in chapter 1), there is often a short period of time when the blockchain splits into two competing chains and two different transaction histories. This happens when two miners find a new block at the same time. Due to very small time delays in the network, some miners see one block, while others see the other.

The question now arises: Which chain is valid? The PoW algorithm prescribes that it must be the longest blockchain (i.e., the one with the most work combined done on it), so the first chain to be extended by having another block added to it will be considered valid. It thus becomes the source of truth, a single blockchain with a single version of transaction history. Through this mechanism, called the Nakamoto Consensus, the network always comes to an agreement about the truth.

The non-central clock created in this way may be inaccurate compared to atomic clocks, but it clearly determines the order of the network's transactions. The proof-of-work algorithm ensures that it is kept running by the miners.

As we saw in the first chapter, miners can extend the blockchain only with valid blocks. To find one, they perform arithmetic operations until a target hash defined by the Bitcoin algorithm is found. At this point, all other hash operations that searched for the solution at the same time are discarded. Then the search for a new block starts all over again.

In the early days of Bitcoin, these operations could be performed on a simple personal computer. But with the increasing growth of the Bitcoin network, the equipment requirements for miners have also risen steadily. Today, only specifically manufactured mining hardware, called ASIC miners, provide the necessary computing power to carry out the energy-intensive computing operations that lead to the creation of new blocks. And so, power consumption, in a way, is proof that the work has been done—that the solution has been found and the block has been mined.

Stake Instead of Work

Bitcoin is considered to be the most secure cryptoasset. To rewrite the current block and attack the Bitcoin network, an attacker must perform approximately the same number of hash operations as were required to create this very block. The more kinetic energy in the form of electricity that has flowed into the production of the block, the more expensive such an attack becomes. High attack resistance is so important because it is the only way to achieve consensus within the Bitcoin network. Nevertheless, Bitcoin is repeatedly accused of wasting energy (more on this in chapter 22).

As an alternative to the energy-intensive proof of work, the concept of proof of stake (PoS), also a consensus mechanism for public blockchains, has been in use for quite some time. Only small and barely relevant blockchains have used it so far. However, the Ethereum community wants to make proof of stake the basis of Ethereum 2.0 (more on this in chapter 20).

Rather than the use of kinetic energy in the form of electricity for consensus-building, the PoS approach uses a deterministic method to choose the creator of the next block, depending on wealth (i.e., the amount of coins they hold), or "stake." In the case of Ethereum, this would be measured using the blockchain's own token, ether. Instead of using "work" in the form of energy, users would put ether up at risk, or stake them, on the blockchain. Anyone who has the amount of ether required for staking could be a validator. During the validation period, the corresponding ether would then be frozen on the blockchain.

With their staked tokens, validators vote for the block they want to see added to the blockchain. Thus, their task is similar to what miners do in the proof-of-work approach. It's just that the validation of new blocks is not done by an extrinsic factor like energy in the case of Bitcoin, but by the blockchain-intrinsic token itself.

In order to motivate users to stake their ether tokens for the validation of new blocks, a reward proportional to the staked amount of ether is being proposed. In the same breath, validators will be punished if they validate forged blocks. This reward-and-punishment system should ensure that validators behave honestly and add only correct blocks to the blockchain.

The Human Factor

Opinions differ as to which consensus mechanism is better. What speaks in favor of proof of work is that it has already proven itself on a global level. It is based on the limited, or constrained, vision of the future described in the previous chapter. Accordingly, restrictions are real and can only be overcome through compromises. One of these limitations, for example, is expressed by the famous Dunbar number—150—which is the limit on the number of stable relationships that an individual can cognitively maintain.

To overcome such limitations, we need institutions that provide social scaling (more on this in chapter 26). However, according to computer expert and legal scholar Nick Szabo, in order to increase social scalability, one must limit technical scalability (i.e., make technology simpler by reducing unneeded complexity).

By using kinetic energy to solve a seemingly pointless cryptographic puzzle, the proof-of-work algorithm keeps a public, global blockchain running that trumps all previously known technologies in terms of social scalability. Thus, the algorithm's success does not lie in its computational efficiency, but in its ability to increase social scalability and create the best possible minimization of trust.

With proof of stake, the Ethereum community is pursuing a solution that requires no major compromises. In line with its unlimited, or unconstrained, vision of the future, it is convinced that social scalability combined with the best possible minimization of trust can also be achieved with computing, and therefore energy efficiency, alone. Ethereum is therefore further developing the relevant cryptographic methods and economic incentives in order to one day, hopefully, implement proof of stake without errors.

Let us be clear: cryptography and economic incentives are also indispensable within the Bitcoin protocol. However, there is another essential element to this protocol that we have not yet mentioned: unforgeable costliness. This term also goes back to Nick Szabo and describes something that is difficult or impossible to forge and at the same time scarce and therefore difficult to obtain.

The concept of unforgeable costliness is best illustrated with gold. This precious metal is said to have been produced during the collision of neutron stars—as human beings, we are currently unable to reproduce it in a laboratory or in a factory. At the same time, no one has yet succeeded in counterfeiting gold. Gold is therefore an unforgeable costly resource.

In contrast to proof of stake, proof of work is based on the principle of unforgeable costliness. By using the component electricity from outside the blockchain to reach a consensus, PoW generates scarcity and also creates an objective frame of reference in the digital world. PoS, on the other hand, is based on subjectivity, striving for a entirely blockchain-intrinsic consensus.

The computational work required in proof of work and the electricity consumed for it eliminate human contribution to the creation and verification of new blocks. It is precisely because Bitcoin is a critical system that such a design approach makes sense. Critical systems are those that are so important that in the event of failure they can endanger the human lives and organizations based on this system.

In Ethereum 2.0 with proof of stake, the possibility of human error is not completely eliminated as a source of error at the level of the consensus mechanism. This makes Ethereum much more susceptible to attacks than

Bitcoin. If, for example, hackers steal the private access keys of several validators, as has already happened with smaller blockchains, they can manipulate the network to their advantage.

In addition, proof of stake runs the risk of being politicized. Validators can potentially be bribed or become involved in all sorts of intrigue, as they would be a prominent target for lobbyists. This would inevitably influence the consensus-building process and could lead to its distortion. In this context, it makes sense for some Bitcoiners to point out that proof of stake is ultimately a concealed form of proof of work. In the latter case, costs occur in the form of electricity; in the former, physical, mental and emotional energies are required to navigate and survive the political labyrinth, which makes this system costly nonetheless.

On the consensus level, Bitcoin may be apolitical, but on the governance level neither Bitcoin nor Ethereum can avoid political disputes about block sizes or updates. And that is good and right: both projects thrive and progress based on competition between the ideas of their supporters.

BRAVE NEW DIGITAL WORLD!
COME WITH ME!
WE'RE VISITING THE FUTURE!
WE'RE IN YEAR 2035.
WHAT'S THAT CHIP ON YOUR CHEST?
A BIO-CHIP COMMUNICATOR. IT HOLDS YOUR DIGITAL IDENTITY AND COMMUNICATES WITH OTHER GADGETS.
To enter the building, we need to access your identity. Do you approve?
YES!
2 sats received. You may now enter, welcome!
THESE PEOPLE ON THE SIDE ARE THE HAVE-NOTS OF CRYPTO SOCIETY AND ARE IN DANGER OF PERISHING.
Entry just 0.1 sats!
DON'T YOU BELONG TO THIS RACE?
A COUPLE SATOSHIS TO SPARE?
IF I COULD ONLY TELL YOU THE WHOLE TRUTH AND LIVE A BETTER LIFE!
...IN A WORLD THAT ACCEPTS AND LOVES THE DIGITAL AND KALI!

Bitcoin has no value! And if it does, then only for criminals, who use it to do drugs and money laundering. It's the biggest of all financial bubbles! This so-called currency is volatile, slow and completely inefficient. It's also very bad for the environment!

Lord IB von Kratz, Comic Figure

22. The Burning Energy Question

Nowadays, manmade climate change is regarded as the greatest threat to humanity. Excessive energy consumption therefore falls under general suspicion, especially when its purpose is not apparent to everyone—as in the case of bitcoin mining, for example.

When given a careful look, it's clear that the consumption of energy is vital for survival. Food intake is nothing other than the supply of energy for the body to do its work. The French mathematician Gaspard-Gustave de Coriolis summed up the relationship between work and energy in the 19th century: Work must be used either to set a body in motion—kinetic energy—or to "charge" it with potential energy, also known as elevation energy. Conversely, a moving or otherwise "charged" body can convert its energy into work.

If we apply this connection to the economic world, it means that we have to use energy to do work to increase prosperity. The standard of living is the result of energy consumption. Of course, a high standard of living does not necessarily have to go hand in hand with high energy consumption, and things are also much more complicated in reality: energy is available in many different forms, there are countless machines, and professions differ greatly from one another. Nevertheless, the processes of economic change can be traced back to the basic relationship proposed by Coriolis.

With this realization in mind, it is not surprising that prosperity and energy consumption are highly correlated. The fact that life in the Western world is so comfortable today from a material point of view is partly due to our relatively high energy consumption. This should not, under any circumstances, trivialize the danger of global warming or be a call to burn unnecessary amounts of fossil fuels that emit carbon dioxide. However, the importance of energy consumption for our prosperity cannot be denied either. This understanding will accompany us throughout the following pages.

The Energy Guzzler

As we saw in the last chapter, mining new bitcoin requires energy. This is why the cryptocurrency is being met with hostility. Critics accuse it of wasting precious energy on solving an infinitely complex mathematical problem just to solve an infinitely complex mathematical problem—an end in itself.

Naturally, Bitcoiners see things differently. The solution to the mathematical puzzle is what gives rise to the scarcity and thus the value of the cryptoasset. The calculations are the digitized version of the search for a needle in a haystack. Due to the algorithmically given "difficulty," it becomes more difficult to find the solution the more miners there are who try to solve the task at the same time.

Miners must execute a hash function millions to billions of times as quickly as possible until one finds the right answer. The probability that a certain miner will find such a hash solution is tiny and varies from calculation to calculation due to the degree of difficulty. But a network participant always finds the solution—on average, every 10 minutes.

This process is of utmost importance for the functionality of Bitcoin; by using energy, miners ensure that the cryptoasset remains functional. The huge hashing power, which causes the large energy consumption, secures the non-central accounting of Bitcoin and makes the cryptocurrency an unforgeable costly product (more on this in chapter 21). As we saw in the previous chapter, Bitcoin's proof-of-work mechanism converts energy into economically valuable trust.

The crypto market currently seems to approve of this process, including its energy consumption. Otherwise, bitcoin would have already crashed. However, it is uncertain what the future holds. After all, it is assumed that Bitcoin will consume more and more energy in the future. It is estimated that it could one day consume more than half of the world's energy. Critics also warn against a climatic Armageddon caused by cryptoassets.

Forecasts, however, should never be taken at face value. All future predictions are inevitably incomplete because they cannot foresee all the variables that make up the world. For example, the progress resulting from new technologies that are still unimaginable today or the discovery of new deposits of raw materials or energy sources can hardly be taken into account.

In addition, processes sometimes change direction. The fact that energy consumption in bitcoin mining is currently rising does not mean that this will always be the case. Energy production technology could change radically, and bitcoin mining could become much more energy-efficient than it is today. Open blockchain advocate Andreas Antonopoulos provided the following analogy of a doctor saying, "Madam, I'm concerned about the progress of your pregnancy. At current rate of growth, your belly will be the size of this building in just 5 years."

Today, due to technological advances, the economic throughput or economic density of a Bitcoin transaction is already increasing without the amount of energy used for it increasing in lockstep. The further the development of Bitcoin progresses, the more economic value it will secure with each and every individual transaction. This should make the Bitcoin network more energy-efficient.

Buyer of Last Resort

Most of Bitcoin's mining facilities are located in China and other countries with comparatively cheap energy. This is why miners are frequently accused of covering their energy requirements primarily by burning coal in these countries.

As profit-oriented commercial enterprises, Bitcoin miners naturally have an interest in procuring their energy where it is cheapest. Because they are geographically independent—after all, they don't have to deliver physical products to local customers—they can ship their computing equipment to places where energy is cheap more easily and quickly than other industries. Where there is an abundance of electricity due to overproduction, this excess energy can be used by Bitcoin before it goes to waste.

In other words, thanks to their high mobility, bitcoin miners graze stranded energy assets in remote locations, transforming them into bitcoin units and "storing" them this way. As such, bitcoin mining can be compared to aluminum production. For example, some 50 years ago, Iceland began to process aluminum ore (bauxite) and export the resulting aluminum. This process is heavily dependent on electricity, which Iceland had in abundance. In this way, aluminum served as a means of "exporting" electricity from a country where this energy resource was plentiful, basically stranded and would have otherwise been lost.

Bitcoin enthusiasts are of course willing to exploit such scenarios and dynamics. They also argue that Bitcoin, as the ultimate energy buyer, can create incentives to encourage the construction of new power plants in remote areas and pay for their operation more quickly. However, there are doubts as to whether this would really happen and whether the new energy plants would be operated in a climate-neutral manner. Also, because the energy market in most countries is highly centralized and regulated, many inefficiencies exist—which even Bitcoin would probably be unable to solve perfectly.

Not least for selfish reasons, the Bitcoin community takes the issue of energy consumption seriously and tries to work toward a greater global distribution of miners. But this is not easy to achieve in the non-central world of Bitcoin, which is not controlled by any authority.

Bitcoin is no champion when it comes to promoting green energy sources. But it appears that the Chinese Bitcoin miners are at least better than their reputations suggest. Most of them are located in Sichuan province, a stronghold of hydroelectric power generation. Thus, contrary to prejudices, the majority of them are likely using clean energy from water for their mining plants.

Now that it is becoming increasingly clear that electricity is replacing oil as the lifeblood of productivity, Bitcoin is a new expression of tokenized energy of the digital era—just as the petrodollar was the expression of the modern industrial age.

THE CRYPTO WINTER
THE CRYPTO MANIACS HAVE BEEN WEAKEND. WE NEED TO STRIKE NOW AND DESTROY THEM COMPLETELY!
LET'S FIND SATOSHI!
THE SEARCH BEGINS...
WE FOUND HIM!
WHAT DO YOU WANT FROM ME?!

Whether fundamental philosophical questions, the clash of different economic schools, a mysterious creation story, unexpected and paradoxical turnarounds or revolutionary future scenarios - the crypto world contains everything!

Kali, Comic Figure

23. Blockchain and the Law

At virtually every blockchain conference, participants sooner or later come to talk about one topic: the lack of legal certainty in the crypto space. In many eyes, it is the biggest impediment to this still-nascent industry. The general sentiment is that the new world of blockchain technology would have a hard time attracting new money and becoming a mass phenomenon without binding, enforceable rules.

Following the ICO hype of 2018, a real competition for ideas on the subject of blockchain technology broke out among lawyers, particularly in Switzerland. Countless papers and theses were published, which were finally included in the 170-page government report released by the Swiss Federal Council in December 2018. Internationally, the report is regarded as a good position statement that shows where action is still needed at the legislative level.

Two decisive questions of a civil law nature must be answered regarding blockchain technology and cryptoassets. First, do crypto tokens constitute property? And second, is Bitcoin a thing? These question the potential physicality of a fully digital application.

In Switzerland, at least, the legal situation seems paradoxical: although Swiss law does not give a clear definition of an object, it is a prerequisite for establishing property. Part of the doctrine is based on the assumption that a thing requires physicality (i.e., that it must be something tangible); however, this would exclude ownership of crypto tokens. But other lawyers interpret the concept of property in a more contemporary way than Eugen Huber, the author of the Swiss Civil Code, was able to do in 1904, in ignorance of digital tokens. In this way, the analysis of property law should not focus on physicality, but on the controllability of the matter at hand.

Not only physical computers and smartphones but also the immaterial software installed on them can be mastered. The same applies to digital tokens based on a blockchain. Thanks to private access keys, only a single person and no one else has control over certain tokens. This gives them property-like qualities, which justifies the use of property rights.

This is particularly important when cryptoassets are held by a third party that files for bankruptcy. Provisions under the law of obligations regarding the segregation of foreign objects say that foreign tokens should be removed from the bankrupt party's estate, provided that the owner can be clearly identified through the blockchain.

Just as important is the question of property law in the transfer of crypto tokens. Within respective blockchain systems, tokens can be transferred comprehensibly for all parties involved at any time. However, since the matter of ownership (and thus also that of transfer) has not yet been conclusively clarified in a legal framework, no definitive transfer can take place from a legal point of view.

In order to legally ensure the change of ownership, Swiss lawyers have examined several related factors: intellectual property, copyright, and securities or book-entry rights laws. However, crypto tokens only partially fulfill their requirements. Therefore, only the law regarding transfers of claims remains; however, Swiss law requires these transfers of claims to be made in written form. So anyone who wants to transfer a token must submit a paper document—which makes no sense at all with digital tokens. Even a digital signature unnecessarily complicates the transfer. This demonstrates the entire difficulty of the current legal debate: the analog legal system is simply not geared toward digital applications.

However, there are approaches to ensure the portability of cryptoassets—and they are also discussed in the Federal Council's report on the legal framework of blockchain technology in Switzerland. One option is to create a new category of digital book-entry rights, the transmission of which would be recorded in a decentralized ledger—a blockchain. This would require an adaptation of the Swiss Code of Obligations.

This would enable an issuer to distribute its asset token as a digital value right via a public blockchain such as Ethereum without having to keep an additional central register, which would no longer be necessary since a public blockchain is already a register, only a decentralized one. Accounting or auditing, for example, would no longer be handled by a central, human-staffed office, but by computers based on mathematics—efficiency gains would be the result.

Tokens Without Counterparties

Utility and payment tokens are the counterparts of asset tokens. While the latter represents rights that exist apart from the blockchain, such as dividend claims and voting rights, and thus have a counterparty, utility and payment tokens usually lack this. Accordingly, crypto tokens can also be divided into tokens with and without counterparties.

Ether is an example of a payment token that also serves as a utility token, through which the Ethereum blockchain can be used. This does not involve interaction with a central counterparty, but with software. Utility and payment tokens do not embody any rights beyond their technical functionality. The legal transfer of such tokens is therefore less problematic.

Nevertheless, established financial circles regularly declare the utility token dead. According to professional investors, it lacks any underlying value. What they do not say is that a security or asset token is easier to integrate into the regulations of the existing system, which is what many people are looking for since their focus is to use blockchain technology for classic and therefore centralized business models.

When it all started with Bitcoin, decentralization was in the foreground. A decentralized structure without a counterparty is the real revolutionary thing about crypto. If a decentralized network creates an increase in demand, its value rises and utility tokens can also be interesting for investors. The value is thus linked to the network and profits from network effects—in contrast to the asset token, whose return always depends on the sales figures of an individual company.

Non-centralized infrastructures without counterparties are still at the very beginning of their development, and many legal challenges are likely to arise in the future. This can be seen in the case of EtherDelta, a supposedly decentralized trading platform for ether and other Ethereum-based tokens. In November 2018, the U.S. Securities and Exchange Commission charged its founder, Zachary Coburn, for operating an unregistered exchange. The decisive factor was that the platform was very similar to a centralized exchange.

There was a central website on which traders' bids ran on a centrally controlled server. The fees were pocketed by EtherDelta's operators, who also decided how high the fees ought to be.

This case does not constitute a precedent when it comes to the essential question of the extent to which a developer of non-central software can be held responsible for its functioning. It shows, however, that many supposedly decentralized applications and protocols are actually not decentralized at all. In such cases, there are obvious starting points from which to apply the applicable laws, whereas no simple framework exists regarding truly non-central blockchain protocols and crypto applications.

The Limits of National Law

Even with traditional, centrally operated online services, it is becoming repeatedly apparent that local, state and centralized laws are reaching their limits. These are practically ineffective against non-central networks, which can evade government legal authority at any time and in which connecting factors can be difficult to establish.

Therefore a user who uses a non-central software protocol or a non-central application is held responsible as the connecting factor instead. Another possible connecting factor is the location of the servers. But these are often rented, distributed worldwide and can hardly be localized. As demonstrated by Satoshi Nakamoto, the anonymous inventor of Bitcoin, the digital world can also lack any trace leading back to the originator of a technology.

Above all, the question of liability is the subject of intense discussion: What if, for example, a blockchain protocol contains an error and leaves the user in the lurch at the wrong moment? Who can and should then be called to account?

Since the users of a public blockchain have not concluded a contract with its developers, it would be difficult to establish liability on the basis of the current legal approach of "liability under contract." In the opinion of some lawyers, it would be different if justified trust on the part of the users has been deliberately abused (i.e., if deliberate false claims have led to disadvantages). In this case, there could be a viable basis for the action. Bitcoin, which is published under the MIT License—which is a free-of-charge, open-source software license created at the Massachusetts Institute of Technology—expressly disclaims any warranty or liability. A further connecting factor is tort law. In order for liability to arise, there must be a duty on the part of the developer that has been violated. Some lawyers believe this obligation arises from the fact that protocol developers offer specialized services. In their opinion, this results in a relationship of trust based on good faith, a kind of trusteeship between the trustee (in this case, the developer) and the trustor (the user), not unlike the relationship between a doctor and their patient.

Other lawyers and open-source developers argue that a doctor is licensed, has fiduciary obligations to only one patient at a time and is paid for their service. In open-source projects, however, developers are not officially licensed and do not provide their services to one specific person. In addition, as we have seen, developers do not have sole control over a public blockchain protocol.

The legal question of liability is just one approach to dealing with public blockchains. Another is self-responsibility, which means bearing the consequences not only of one's own commitments and promises, but also of one's own mistakes and errors. Personal responsibility radically questions the legal monopoly of the state. If all people were to act based on their own responsibility, the traditional and reactive legal system would be superfluous. By allowing public blockchains to give more justice to individual responsibility, we can ideally proclaim a new legal order.

The Digital Good

From a legal point of view, Bitcoin has also ushered in a new era because it treats the concept of property differently. As history teaches us, property has evolved over the past millennia as an important, and perhaps even the most important, category of law. Without property, the development of human civilization would not have been possible. It is a prerequisite for cooperation, a market economy and, ultimately, prosperity. Particularly since the emergence of nation states, property has been a legal concept defined and enforced by territorial sovereignty. Today it is taken for granted that anyone who wants to assert and enforce property rights against others needs the state to do so.

With the advent of the internet, a new type of product emerged: the digital good. Suddenly, it became possible to own a digital photo album, a website, an email address and even objects within a game. What all these products have in common is that they are neither exclusive nor rivaled in consumption, so everyone has access to every product, which is available in any number.

But Bitcoin changed that. As a digital bearer instrument, the cryptocurrency is the world's first digital private property. Whoever has the private access keys to the corresponding bitcoin has de facto (but not necessarily de jure) ownership of them. Thanks to the invention of digital scarcity combined with asymmetric cryptography, bitcoin is non-centralistic property that exists entirely independently of any state jurisdiction and its law.

Property rights are no longer tied exclusively to a legal system and a monopoly on the use of force. Individuals can now own property that does not depend on enforcement and protection by territorial sovereignty. Values are no longer just physical artifacts but pure information. This, in turn, is likely to have far-reaching legal implications.

Digital information is radically different from physical objects. They are easy to encrypt, can be quickly disassembled into individual parts and reassembled. Information can also be transmitted in a variety of ways, immediately checked for authenticity and hidden in plain sight. Examples are known of people "storing" their private access keys in paintings. Since data do not possess any physicality per se, they can take on almost any form.

Though bitcoin exist as unmistakable units, they are hardly tangible even in a non-physical sense. Due to the non-central character of its blockchain, bitcoin units are nowhere and everywhere at the same time. And by memorizing the private access key, they can be taken anywhere. But without the respective private key, while the bitcoin are still visible on the blockchain, they are no longer accessible and thus actually nonexistent.

In view of these values consisting of zeros and ones, many previously functional laws have reached their limits. The invention of the computer has paved the way for the abstract world of information. And the internet has linked these computers together to form a global, borderless network. With the advent of the so-called trustnet, digital information becomes an exclusively controllable value thanks to cryptography—beyond state and law.

SOMETHING UNIMAGINABLE
ZSCHH-ZZIP!
WITH BLOCKCHAIN WE'VE FOUND A TECHNOLOGY LIKE THE ELECTRICITY OR THE INTERNET.
YOU'RE WRONG! IT'S EVEN MORE...
WHAT DO YOU MEAN?
CORPORATIONS, MARKETS, COUNTRIES - THE BLOCKCHAIN WILL CHANGE EVERYTHING AT ITS FOUNDATIONAL STRUCTURE!
THIS IS WHY BLOCKCHAIN IS AN INSTITUTIONAL TECHNOLOGY!
SO, YOU MEAN THAT EVEN CRYPTO SECESSIONS WOULD BE POSSIBLE?
YES, THAT AND...
...DIGITAL NATIONS MAY ARISE!
EVA, WAIT!
EVERYTHING IS POSSIBLE, KALI!
BUT THIS BLOWS MY IMAGINATION, EVA!

Bitcoin and Blockchain combine a multitude of complex topics: cryptography, computer science, economics, politics, philosophy and biology.

Jay, Comic Figure

24. Cryptoeconomics and Blockchain Governance

Anyone who listens to a discussion between crypto enthusiasts and established economists will soon notice that these two camps are miles apart. Star economists like Paul Krugman, Nouriel Roubini, Joseph Stiglitz and Robert Shiller never miss an opportunity to pick Bitcoin to pieces.

Of course, it is not forbidden to utter criticism. What is noticeable, however, is that all too often in their tirades, scholarly economists lack an understanding of the matter at hand, and their explanations miss the larger picture. Reading Satoshi Nakamoto's white paper on Bitcoin, one immediately notices that there was a systematic thinker at work, who takes into consideration economic as well as psychological and sociological elements. Therefore, it is not surprising that the field of cryptoeconomics is a highly interdisciplinary science.

This new field of research, which deals with the crypto world, combines classical economics with aspects of applied cryptography and game theory. Other areas include computer science, network theory, mechanism design and incentive theory. Its aim is to describe and understand novel emergent systems, applications and networks based on blockchain technology through the study of economic incentives and cryptographic formulas.

As we have already seen, the functionality of Bitcoin is based on the two incentive elements of reward and cost. On the one hand, rewards in the form of bitcoin units ensure that users maintain the network. On the other hand, costs make harmful behavior expensive.

Asymmetric cryptography and hash functions make it possible for economic incentive systems to be built digitally in the first place. Without cryptographically secure ownership of scarce bitcoin tokens, no miner would do their job because they could not be rewarded for it. Without mining, the system would not be safe from attacks, and it would collapse in a very short time.

The combination of incentives and cryptography is immensely important for Bitcoin. While the economic incentives encourage all participants to behave honestly within the network, the cryptographic mechanisms secure peer-to-peer communication within the network.

Asymmetric cryptography is one of the few areas in which defenders have a strong advantage over attackers. An asymmetric key pair of public and private keys cannot be cracked with the computing power available today. The use of asymmetric cryptography goes back to the philosophy of the cypherpunks, who advocated the use of cryptography and technology to better protect the privacy and autonomy of the individual.

In the eyes of Vitalik Buterin and Vlad Zamfir, two of the main faces behind the ongoing development of Ethereum, cryptoeconomic concepts should primarily serve to design protocols that regulate the production, distribution and consumption of goods and services in a non-central, digital economy. For them, cryptoeconomics is therefore a practical science intended to bring about the economic interaction of non-trusting parties.

This is done in particular through mechanism design, which can be seen as the reversal of game theory procedures. One begins with a desired result and then works backward in terms of design. The corresponding parameters are set in such a way that even if the participants acting via this protocol pursue only their own interests, the desired result is nevertheless achieved.

According to Buterin and Zamfir, cryptoeconomic design approaches should be applied at all levels, be it in the elaboration of a functioning consensus mechanism on the basis layer, or in second-layer applications in which well-thought-out smart contracts in particular should play an essential role. It is also important to ensure cryptoeconomically that incentive structures guarantee smooth cooperation between the individual layers and that people are properly incentivized at every level.

Critics, however, object: human beings are not deterministic in any way—how they react to incentive structures can never be predicted perfectly. In this respect, cryptoeconomic design also has its limits. In the eyes of critics, cryptoeconomics is more of a descriptive than a prescriptive undertaking. Rather than applying classical economic theory to crypto networks and assets, the study of cryptoeconomics describes and studies the human actions that, in combination with cryptographic tools, has led to the spontaneous emergence of crypto networks such as Bitcoin. As an institution, Bitcoin is an independently self-regulating entity that grows from within. It emerged from a social process, led by a small group of individuals who drove Bitcoin forward with their actions. And although each and every individual consciously worked toward the dissemination of the cryptocurrency, the social process of discovery and imitation was neither organized nor is it complete.

In this respect, Bitcoin is also not a decentralized autonomous organization, or DAO, although it is repeatedly described as such. A DAO can be best described as a group of people who work on the basis of cryptographic tokens and transparent software rules and who are not regulated by formal contracts. Unlike traditional companies, DAOs are not managed on a hierarchical and therefore centralistic structure, but jointly on the basis of self-executing smart contracts on the blockchain.

In contrast, Bitcoin was not organized. It is also not decentralized but non-centralized, and therefore cannot be organized (more in chapter 1). Bitcoin is more of an emergent institution than an established organization.

A Question of Leadership

Due to their global, permissionless character, crypto networks unite people with different views. The differences are particularly evident when it comes to the further development of the respective networks. Over the past 10 years, Bitcoiners have fought several battles. The most prominent was the block size debate, which led to a hard fork and split the Bitcoin community apart (read more in chapter 18).

Ethereum also experienced a governance crisis. In May 2016, a project called The DAO was launched on its blockchain, the first of these decentralized autonomous organizations, in this case an independent venture capital fund on the blockchain. Only a few weeks later, a vulnerability in the smart-contract code was discovered and exploited. Approximately one-third of the funds held in ether were drained—and this was a legitimate action because it corresponded to the code.

The Ethereum community nevertheless decided to subject the blockchain to a hard fork in order to return the "stolen" ether to its original owners. This incident is the reason why the Ethereum community is split today and why Ethereum Classic, the original blockchain, exists alongside the main blockchain. Bitcoin's block size debate and Ethereum's DAO fiasco have been used again and again to argue for a clearer and more formal governance of blockchain networks. While the Ethereum community began to discuss governance models more intensively, Bitcoiners seemed to think such a discussion was less necessary in the case of their cryptocurrency.

Two levels of governance are distinguished: protocol and social. On the protocol level, the blockchain nodes create consensus, and this governance is algorithmic and strictly on-chain. This type of consensus is also called ledger consensus. Discussions on issues such as the modification of the blockchain protocol are shifted to the societal level and take place off-chain: in forums, on social media or at conferences. This kind of consensus building can also be called social consensus.

In the case of Bitcoin, the unwritten law of the so-called rough consensus applies: changes are proposed as software updates, and the entire ecosystem discusses which updates should be adopted. Proposals are rolled over until the majority is convinced that they are useless. If this agreement is not reached, the community continues to pursue the idea that might actually one day change the Bitcoin protocol.

The lack of formal governance sometimes leads to the escalation of discussions and debates. In other cases, when the community seems to agree and the risk of hard forks is low, the changes are implemented quickly. Many crypto enthusiasts—but also exponents outside the crypto world—do perceive this type of decision-making as opaque and chaotic.

Moreover, core developers often seem to be in control, even if they have no formal authority to be so. A closer look appears to confirm this impression. Only five core developers—also known as maintainers—hold "commit access keys," which would allow them to change the Bitcoin source code.

But they don't have a clear run. As a global phenomenon, Bitcoin is under the constant supervision of many people who know just as much about software and programming as the maintainers do. Therefore, it has happened time and again that the core developers' suggestions for changes were rejected by the community. Although these core developers could change the Bitcoin program code on their own, this would be devastating for them since other developers could easily fork the Bitcoin code, and the maintainers would then no longer have access to the new blockchain.

Core developers are not the gatekeepers of Bitcoin. Like language, Bitcoin is a social, emergent phenomenon. Although there are repeated attempts to influence a language via legal writer reforms, consensus on the meaning of words is ultimately reached organically. The same applies to Bitcoin.

But those outside the Bitcoin community do not seem to accept the rationale above. As critics say: off-chain governance allows individual and sometimes shady parties to exert influence. For this reason, many Bitcoin proponents advocate for on-chain solutions: direct votes on the blockchain should answer governance questions of all kinds.

The Tezos blockchain demonstrates how this could work. Its base layer contains a process that allows stakeholders, or "bakers," to vote on-chain on changes to the protocol or governance process. Developers put any intended source code changes to the vote, allowing bakers to vote on them. A Tezzie, the Tezos token, represents a vote. To implement a proposal, at least 80 percent of the voters must agree.

Proponents of on-chain governance see this standardized procedure as desirable because changes are transparent and democratic. Once a change is approved, all network nodes automatically upgrade. Forks therefore become a thing of the past. Critics of this approach regard the procedure as problematic—if upgrades are always performed the same way, network nodes lose their veto, so to speak.

Attempts at on-chain governance are still in their infancy. It is probably still too early to make a definite judgment about their functionality and usefulness. But today, public choice theory provides us with interesting insights into the pitfalls of collective decision-making.

For example, the American economist Mancur Olson examined both the power of interest groups and the collective action problem—a situation in which individuals would benefit from coordinated action, but fail to take such action because from an individual's point of view they do not have sufficient incentives to actually cooperate. The consequence is that individuals are less well organized than small interest groups, which regularly puts the former at a disadvantage in political disputes. This fate could also befall blockchain users if smaller groups exploit the governance structures for their own benefit.

Moreover, public governance structures tend toward a rent-seeking economy. This refers to the process in which individuals increase their prosperity without creating new wealth or giving back a benefit to society. Inflation profiteers such as miners or validators, for example, have an incentive to maximize inflation. They could become political actors who influence other blockchain users so that they vote in their favor. Lobbying, buying votes and clientelization would be the inevitable consequences—precisely those things that public blockchains want to avoid. Political economists have also found out that the rules of a voting system influence the election result of a vote. Often, voters are asked to simply say "yes" or "no" to an update. The "yes, but" or "no, but" camps are not heard. This of course can lead to social unrest and distort the structure around a public blockchain project. And it raises the question of whether a long debate, in which at least all voices can have their say, is not the better governance mechanism.

The Bitcoin community, for its part, wants to leave the system as designed by Satoshi Nakamoto. What might sound like quasireligious conviction is in reality merely a way to show appreciation to the systematic thinking that the anonymous Bitcoin inventor demonstrated in his active time. Some Bitcoiners therefore believe it makes sense to ossify the base layer of the blockchain (i.e., so that it can no longer be changed). Of course, this does not apply to other layers and applications.

DEFI'S ROBO ADVISOR
WE NEED MORE FUNDING.
WE DON'T GET FURTHER LOANS FROM BANKS!
YES, WE STRUGGLE LIKE ALL STARTUPS!
I'VE LISTEN TO YOUR CONVERSATION.
...I HAVE SOME NEAT OFFERS FOR YOU. NO BANKS INVOLVED, ONLY SOURCE CODE AND PROTOCOLS.
WHAT ARE YOUR NEEDS, COLATERALS AND INVESTMENT HORIZONT?
HOW COMPLICATED IS THIS WHOLE THING?
I'VE ALREADY AUTHENTICATED YOU WITH YOUR DIGITAL IDENTITY. AND THE PROTOCOLS ARE INTEROPERABLE. RUNS ALL OVER THE BLOCKCHAIN.
WOW! THAT'S JUST THE TICKET!
WHAT ELSE DO YOU NEED? FOR EXAMPLE A COMPLETE OVERVIEW OF YOUR CRYPTO PORTFOLIO?
KALI, LOOK. THE WORLD OF DECENTRALIZED FINANCIAL OFFERS SIMPLE LENDINGS OVER A MONEY PROTOCOL WITHOUT ANY BANKS INVOLVED. SMART AND BETTER THAN IN THE TRADITIONAL WORLD.
EVERYTHING IS CONFIRMED. THE CRYPTOASSETS ARE ALREADY IN YOUR DIGITAL WALLET!

We are in an exciting era, where technology will change banking and its processes. Change offers opportunities for people and companies that think and act entrepreneurially in the new field of tokenized products or smart contracts.

Marianne Wildi, CEO Hypothekarbank Lenzburg

25. The Token Economy

Tokens here, tokens there. In the course of the crypto euphoria triggered by Bitcoin, digital tokens have sprung up like mushrooms and seem to have ushered in the age of the token economy.

The term *token economy* dates back to the 19th century and originally comes from psychology. It describes a system of incentives designed to strengthen and promote desirable behavior. Behavioral economics adopted the model and applied it primarily in laboratory experiments to simulate human decision-making in economic contexts.

The new crypto tokens are intended to put this concept of the token economy into practice and thus into the real world. Its proponents hope that it will create incentives where they are missing and correct ones that are distorted to bring better harmony to the market. The token economy is supposed to be the market economy 2.0, so to speak.

Markets have always enabled the voluntary exchange of goods and services between buyers and sellers. For transactions to take place between market participants, the parties involved must have at least some degree of trust in each other. Intermediaries most commonly take care of this, bringing the parties together and guaranteeing a relationship of mutual trust.

The simplest example of such an intermediary might be an operator of a marketplace, who, on the one hand, ensures fair competition between traders and, on the other hand, informs customers about market days. A more complex form of intermediary is an investment bank that supports a startup company in its IPO.

Intermediaries are indispensable for the functioning of markets. As the size of trading venues increases, so does the importance of intermediaries. Of course, they try to profit as much as possible with their services, but as long as the verification costs remain lower than the benefits that market participants derive from interaction, trading on the marketplace will continue to take place.

The token economy integrates verification and auditing into public blockchains. This makes free verification possible, which theoretically makes intermediaries superfluous. Advocates of the new token economy see this development as an opportunity to break up monopolistic platforms such as those of the tech giants and replace them with token-based networks. The token plays a central role here. As a value unit of a network, it is part of the incentive structure: the token owner is financially involved in the network and has an interest in its success, since they profit from it. This way, users of the network—be they developers, marketers or sellers—contribute to the further proliferation and success of the network and the token economy.

In addition, growing user numbers strengthen the network: on the one hand, it becomes more decentralized and secure, and on the other hand, participants work to improve the network and offer new services on top of it. This network effect increases the benefits of the system, which in turn attract new users—creating a self-reinforcing feedback loop.

While existing systems are driven by a simple network effect, public blockchains benefit from a new kind of network effect: the network owner effect. This new incentive structure is expected to redefine the essence of online networks and internet communities. As we have already seen in chapter 10, before the rise of the new token economy, it was quite difficult to make money developing new internet protocols. But tokens enable internet ownership. And they allow their creators to monetize blockchain protocols directly. The network owner effect not only creates new economic incentives for network growth and the ability to monetize protocols, but it also aligns the goals of all parties involved in the network, as each user is also a co-owner of the network.

With existing internet platforms, including the so-called sharing economy, this is hardly the case; a majority of users are faced with a minority of owners. Jeffrey Wernick, an early Bitcoin investor, pointed out that the value of the ridesharing service Uber, for example, is increasing at the same rate that drivers' wages are falling. In his opinion, a true sharing economy can only be ushered in through tokenization.

Tokenization of the Real World

Bitcoin and other cryptoassets are digital tokens. So, will the advantages of the token economy be limited only to the digital world?

To answer this question, it helps to examine the concept of fungibility. On a public blockchain like Ethereum, fungible as well as non-fungible tokens can be created today. A token is fungible if it can be replaced by another token of the same type. Probably the most intuitive example is a banknote in your wallet. Five U.S. dollars can be exchanged with any other five-dollar bill in order to buy goods worth five dollars.

A non-fungible token, on the other hand, is uniquely identifiable and basically not divisible. It differs from any other token. Although non-fungible tokens belong to the same class, they are not the same. A non-fungible token can therefore be associated with anything that has non-fungible properties. This is where tokenization of the real world comes into play, since the world consists of innumerable non-fungible goods. Through tokenization, objects in the real world can receive a digital counterpart and thus be mapped in cyberspace.

However, objects such as real estate or paintings do not have to be represented solely by one non-fungible token but can also be represented by several tokens at once. These tokens are fungible, or interchangeable, with each other, but are non-fungible with respect to "outside" tokens that are non-similar or represent a different asset.

There is also a distinction between indivisible and divisible tokens. A token is indivisible if it exists only as a whole token and cannot be broken down into smaller units. A divisible token, on the other hand, is fractional and can be divided into smaller pieces. One bitcoin, for example, is divisible to the eighth decimal place (i.e., can be divided into 100 million satoshis). ERC20 tokens, the standard for Ethereum tokens, can usually be divided up to 18 decimal places.

The tokenization of real estate in particular is currently a source of enthusiasm. Until now, investors have been able to invest in real estate only if they either acquired a property directly or participated in a real estate company or a fund. A direct investment requires not only capital, but also time and knowledge. First you have to find the right property, followed by the search for the best mortgage, conclusion of the contract, land registration, administration, tax planning, choice of legal form and dealings with local authorities—there is a lot to do and even more to consider.

An indirect investment can delegate these challenges, but there is a lack of individualization, transparency and converging interests. This is why blockchain technology is now being used in the real estate industry to leverage investments and to make processes more efficient. By digitally mapping real estate as non-fungible tokens, related titles and documents can also be stored on the blockchain and signed using smart contracts.

On Ethereum, for example, a property can be tokenized using an ERC20 token created by means of a smart contract and offered for sale to investors via a platform. Any number of tokens can be issued per object. Since the purchase of a single token is sufficient for participation in the investment, tokenization is intended to democratize real estate investments: less solvent investors should also be able to invest their money in real estate in the future.

With the purchase of a token, an investor acquires a share in the property and can participate in its value creation and development. This is no different than with the purchase of a share, which pays dividends in case of profit. Comparably, a token owner receives a share of the rental income of the property proportional to their share. If the property gains in value, the token price rises and the buyer benefits again.

Tokenization is not only intended to give the broader public access to real estate investments, but it is also intended to make individual real estate investments more liquid. The token shares in a property can be easily sold at any time—without agreements with co-owners, pre-emptive rights or changes in the land register, which are still common on conventional real estate platforms today.

Tokenization is met with excitement because it weakens the dominance of the traditional banking and investment world. On the one hand, real estate, works of art or luxury vehicles can be tokenized comparatively easily thanks to the blockchain. On the other hand, people who previously did not have bank accounts or the necessary funds for big investments will be able to use the blockchain.

However, Bitcoin enthusiasts in particular are critical of tokenization. They fear that it will distract from the real problem, the ongoing creation of money within our system, which has caused asset prices to explode. In the eyes of Bitcoiners, tokenization could even exacerbate the problem, as it taps into previously untapped liquidity reserves and thus promotes the unhealthy financialization of the world. As Bitcoiners argue, the fact that tokenization is also being promoted for goods such as artwork and other items that do not generate passive returns is connected to today's enormous expansion of money. If it weren't for today's age of devaluation, when savers are given a very hard time, art and other luxury goods would not have turned into extravagant monetary investments to the extent that they have. Trying to make these goods more liquid through tokenization is just a way to put the cart before the horse.

But this is by no means the only criticism. Tokenization also brings with it very practical problems, such as when forks occur on the corresponding blockchain. In the case of a fork, two different tokens would suddenly make demands on the same asset, and someone would have to make a decision about which claim is legitimate. Of course, such an eventuality could be regulated in a contract, which could even be hashed into a public blockchain (i.e., stored in a way that cannot be changed). If a legal dispute arises, reference can be made to the hash stored in the smart contract, which represents the real contract and can be clearly identified.

In this way, a legally effective connection can be established between the blockchain and the physical world. This means, however, that one would have to resort to a central legal entity—which the crypto world is currently trying to circumvent. Therefore, it might make much more sense to operate tokenization on a sidechain such as the Liquid network right from the beginning (see chapter 19).

Back to Barter

One of the most interesting aspects of tokenization has not yet been addressed. In combination with increasingly powerful artificial intelligence, it could lead to the rebirth of the barter economy—in the form of what economist Chris Berg and Jason Potts call " high-frequency barter trading".

Direct bartering, as we know from economics textbooks, is subject to scaling problems. If you want to exchange something, your ability to do so isn't simply dependent on finding someone who has what you want. It is also dependent on what you have to offer and what your potential exchange partner is looking for. This double agreement of wants can only be found, if at all, in very small communities.

As soon as an economy adopts what is called the division of labor, direct bartering quickly becomes too costly. It becomes costly to impossible for a single person to find suitable barter partners. As a result, money that enables indirect exchange becomes more attractive.

Tokenization makes physical goods digitally tradable, increasing their liquidity. By tokenizing all kinds of physical goods and storing them on a blockchain, they can be exchanged, bought and sold more easily. Artificial intelligence can help in this regard too. It can analyze large data sets much faster than human beings. Without incurring large costs, they can amass a huge range of tokenized assets and determine advantageous barter transactions. The tokenized world of tomorrow could therefore be a world in which consumers, companies and other participants have all sorts of money-like assets—tokens—at their disposal, which could be traded almost completely and without friction costs.

So far, trade is confined to binary trading pairs. Tokenized assets, however, can be aggregated into trade sequences of many different trading pairs, making barter an efficient method of transacting. Because of blockchain technology trading can be atomic, trades don't follow what is called delivery versus payment (DVP), where the transfer of a good or security only happens after payment has been made. In what can be called a location swap, goods can be moved without having to actually physically move them. In what can be called a location swap, goods can be moved without having to actually physically move them. In a token swap, merely the claims to the corresponding assets are exchanged; this way, more is accomplished with less. Through tokenization, the Uberization of trading is becoming a reality: just as Uber does not have to own any cars to transport people, tokenizing assets allows for exchange without movement.

Interestingly enough, that the gap between the analog and digital worlds is likely to be closed in the future is a plausible assumption given today's technological progress. The internet of things or nanoparticles will one day be able to connect physical objects with each other (see chapter 17). Blockchain technology will allow for the use tokens—acting as unforgeable and unambiguously identifiable digital representations of physical objects—that are easier to trade or exchange.

In this way, an independent and autonomous machine economy should gradually emerge, a machine-to-machine, instead of today's peer-to-peer, ledger. Looking into the distant future, there are already some cunning observers who argue that blockchain technology and tokenization are not meant primarily for us human beings, but ultimately for the machines and digital personalities of the future. But only this future will show what kinds of consequences this will have for the financial sector, monetary policy, the economy and the global distribution of property rights.

HARD TO KILL!
EVEN MORE BLOCKCHAINS AND SIDECHAINS ARISE
THESE THINGS ARE GROWING LIKE WEEDS. WE NEED TO TAKE THIS FIGHT TO THE MAX!
LORD IB VON KRATZ, OUR PRISONER IS NOT SATOSHI!
WHAT!? HOW MUCH BAD NEWS DO I NEED TO ENDURE! TAKE THEM DOWN!!!
EVERYWHERE, COMPUTERS ARE BEING DESTROYED.
...BUT THE BLOCKCHAIN IS TOO ROBUST AND CANNOT BE DESTROYED.

Technological progress forces us to critically question our relationships of trust time and again. In the context of "Distributed Ledger Technology", the question even poses itself if complete decentralization is the gravediggers of trust due to the lack of tangible anchor points.

Patrick Hunger, Attorney at Law

26. Capitalism After Satoshi

Institutions consist of three basic building blocks: technology, incentives and the human element. The combination of these three components creates trust. In traditional institutions such as industrial companies or states, the human element weighs most heavily. Bitcoin, in contrast, reduces the human element to an unprecedented extent and gives greater weight to the other two components. On the one hand, incentives (as we have seen in chapter 24) are intended to keep the human element in check; on the other hand, mathematics, cryptography and computer science are intended to make technology more complex and crucial.

When traditional companies today talk about integrating blockchain technology into their systems, they expect this to lead to efficiency gains, that existing structures and interfaces will be optimized. In the eyes of many crypto enthusiasts, however, such a focus does not do justice to the new technology. The blockchain is not merely a new information and communication technology to increase the efficiency of business processes. Rather, it is a new carrier technology, also known as general-purpose technology, whose significance is comparable with electricity, transistors, computers, smartphones or the internet.

The blockchain could even prove to be a new institutional technology. Carrier technologies enable an economy as a whole to do work better, faster and cheaper. In this respect, carrier technologies act as engines of economic growth. Institutional technologies have an even more fundamental impact.

They transform institutions and thus the structures of trust within the economy and society. As a result, the way in which we interact with other people, and thus the appearance of our economy, changes.

Our present economic system is the product of a development process that has been ongoing for thousands of years. It is characterized by the desire to create mutual trust and thus reduce transaction costs in human interactions. This has been achieved with the help of formal and informal institutions. The former includes constitutions, laws, treaties and organizations, while the latter includes social norms, customs and traditions.

Simplified, the history of humanity could thus be described as a never-ending attempt to establish institutionalized trust structures for mutual cooperation. Mutual trust is the prerequisite for cooperation, and cooperation is the prerequisite for division of labor. This in turn is the reason for our prosperity.

The building of trust began with hunters and gatherers in clan communities. Trust was placed in other clan members and was secured through social pressure or even brute force. Not only did the prehistoric human not trade with other clans, but they were even in constant feud with each other. Bartering took place only within one's own clan.

After the Agricultural Revolution, a large portion of mankind settled down, cultivated crops and raising livestock. So-called hydraulic empires, considered the first advanced civilizations—including Mesopotamia and Ancient Egypt—emerged. Networks of hydraulic engineering plants around the Euphrates, Tigris and Nile rivers created hierarchical societies managed by centralized hands.

Greek and later Roman culture somewhat broke up this hydraulic-controlled and hierarchically organized form of society. Encouraged by Roman law and spurred by precious metals and numerous forms of credit, cooperation between foreigners (i.e., non-clan members) took shape for the first time. Slavery continued to be an important economic institution—the latifundia of ancient Rome were large agricultural estates on which the work was performed by slaves.

The Middle Ages and the transition to modern times created new forms of institutionalized trust. The three-field system, in particular, an agricultural method in which a third of the land lay fallow to recover, was extremely capital-intensive by the standards of the time, and it could not be sustained without cooperation. This led to the creation of the commons, areas of agricultural land used according to jointly agreed rules. Medieval Western Europe was characterized, above all, by the fact that the so-called tragedy of the commons (in this context, the overuse of farmland) was the least prevalent in comparison to other places around the world.

Meanwhile, the guild system was developed in the cities. Guilds were associations of craftsmen and merchants that facilitated the practice of their craft and trade. They formed a socioeconomic system for regulating economic activity. Merchants' guilds joined forces to reduce the cost of long-distance trade negotiations. They created commercial law, which became the basis of confidence for European trade and made trade possible over ever greater distances.

Trade bills and paper loans not only favored long-distance trade but also produced the first banks in northern Italy and a little later in Holland. These were to play a major role, especially during the period of industrialization. As forerunners of today's investment banks, they financed major projects—private and later government paper currencies played a crucial role in this. As the largest shareholders of joint-stock companies, these investment banks paved the way financially for industrial corporations. The company was born as a new structure of trust.

With the transition to the modern age, an uncanny dynamic unfolded, and people were taken by surprise by the explosion in prosperity. After all, according to the history books, 97 percent of our current prosperity is due to this change of course at the beginning of the 19th century. The wealth per capita is said to have increased by a factor of 14 between 1800 and 2000.

It is therefore only logical that people should demand institutionalized law and order in the form of state bureaucracies (also trust structures) to protect their property. Industrialists, bankers, politicians and civil servants made a name for themselves as figureheads of this period. Since they were mutually dependent, these different roles were often fulfilled by one and the same person.

Then the two World Wars interrupted the project of "scaling confidence" and threw progress back again. It was only in the 1990s that international trade was said to have returned to the same scale as before World War One—an indication that the numerous institutionalized structures of trust had yet to prove themselves again. The internet era began around the same time. With the World Wide Web, a new digital world started to grow: global interaction was simplified and accelerated many times over, and government fiat currencies began to take on an electronic form, orchestrated by central banks intervening in the financial markets.

In the meantime, the internet and increasingly the analog world are dominated by a handful of technology giants such as Google, Amazon and Facebook. The dominance of these supercorporations is unprecedented to date in economic history, and they are less and less able to obscure that they are primarily pursuing their own interests.

The fact that we as humanity are standing where we are today can be attributed to our seemingly limitless abstraction potential—which distinguishes us from all other living beings on earth—and to our ability to produce ever more enabling technologies. Among them are numerous general-purpose technologies such as the steam engine, electricity and the computer, as well as institutional technologies such as markets, companies and nation states.

Over the past 200 years, while many new general-purpose technologies have established themselves and brought many changes, little has changed fundamentally when it comes to institutional technologies. Companies and nation states still play an important role, and one could even argue that they have never been more essential.

Fundamental Changes

Markets are generally decentralized and emerge spontaneously. Companies are the opposite. They are organized hierarchically, no different from governmental structures. The British economist Dennis Robertson summarized this circumstance, observing that throughout the economy, firms are like "islands of conscious power in this ocean of unconscious cooperation like lumps of butter coagulating in a pail of buttermilk."

Centralist structures emerged in a decentralized market economy because of production costs on the one hand and transaction costs on the other. Thanks to technological progress, production costs fell during industrialization. Greater numbers of actors entered production, expecting to get a piece of the cake. The resulting competitive pressure forced companies to specialize more and more.

But sooner or later, this inevitably led to an increase in transaction costs, especially information and coordination costs, and hierarchies developed to defuse these costs. In the analog age, a hierarchically managed organization could identify potential, obtain information, coordinate and negotiate more quickly than a loose group of individuals could.

From a blockchain perspective, we can picture today's companies as centralized networks of contracts and capital for the production of goods and services. Every financial change in the company is accounted for in a ledger. Blockchains should start here as non-central ledgers. Disintermediation could lead not only to a loss of importance of intermediaries, but also to the de-hierarchization of companies within the economic system. Decentralized markets would be supplemented by decentralized enterprises.

The blockchain does what prices do in markets, contracts in companies, and laws within the realm of government: create trust and minimize transaction costs. When information is readily available and transaction costs fall, the number of profitable peer-to-peer transactions without intermediaries increases. Hierarchically organized organizations that exist only to minimize transaction costs become less profitable and shrink. The world after Satoshi Nakamoto is therefore nothing less than a completely renewed economic and social structure.

As the Bitcoinization of the world progresses, new economies will emerge on blockchains. One example is the kids' economy. Today, children and young people already know how to acquire virtual goods through in-app purchases. Gamers are also familiar with game currencies such as Fortnite V-Bucks and WoW Gold. Children like to earn their own money, but today they have hardly any opportunities to do so. Cryptocurrencies—especially anonymous ones (more on this in chapter 29)—could turn the tide.

Crypto wallets do not require bank accounts and in certain cases do not require identity and legitimation checks. Once user-friendliness is established, children will soon discover this new world. And once they have entered it, or grown up in it, they are unlikely to entrust their money to centralized financial service providers, which they will consider just as lame and outdated as linear television and radio.

According to Bitcoin enthusiasts, banking will be the first area to be deinstitutionalized on a large scale. Even today, software and algorithms are turning banking into apps. When deinstitutionalization progresses as planned, apps will no longer be based on companies but on crypto networks. The changes are likely to take place step by step. First, the Bitcoin Lightning Network will increasingly take away from the payment function of banks. With payments falling away, people will see no reason to keep their money in the banks. This will have other far-reaching consequences. After all, for many people, their checking account is also their savings account, or the two are linked with each other. Without customers' savings deposits, it will become increasingly difficult for banks to grant loans. Banks would shrink to vaults holding jewelry, precious metals, securities and, ironically, Bitcoin access keys.

All of this sounds rather terrifying. Has the last hour come for companies, banks and bureaucracies? As transaction costs fall, the blockchain indeed becomes a more efficient ledger than companies and bureaucracies. But the latter two are not just ledgers, but ledger keepers. Centralized accountants not only bring dependencies, but undoubtedly also advantages. Customers, for example, have a counterparty whom they can ask for help or sue legally. In a future crypto world, this counterparty would no longer exist. On the other hand, the abolition of transaction costs leads to other types of uncertainty.

Similar objections can be formulated with regard to a complete de-hierarchization, which would create new inefficiencies. Experience with decentralized decision-making, flat hierarchies and personal responsibility shows that it is predominantly the agile and flexible organizations that are placing decision-making power in the hands of a few.

At the same time, numerous people seem to be satisfied with giving up responsibility and hiding in the corporate hierarchy from the adversities of the competitive market. The autonomy and freedom offered by Bitcoin and other blockchains are accompanied by the burden of responsibility. Established institutions are the entities to which some people are only too happy to delegate responsibility and where they find comfort and security—some more, others less. To a certain extent, this is part of human nature.

Hierarchically well-ordered systems not only provide support, but also create belonging and identity. This is one of the greatest challenges for crypto networks. Due to their non-centrality, there are fewer points of reference and contact. Ironically, the remaining human element—where it still exists—counteracts this (for example, in the form of influential heads within the community who create identification).

With the publication of the Bitcoin white paper, Satoshi Nakamoto nevertheless ushered in a new era. As a new institutional technology, the blockchain is likely to create new institutionalized trust structures that will challenge existing ones in the long run.

But we are still in the discovery phase. Entrepreneurs and investors are only just beginning to find out which blockchain protocols will one day win the race. Time will tell whether that is Bitcoin, Ethereum or many others. Accordingly, it is still difficult to evaluate real use cases—after all, we are used to assessing entrepreneurial innovation against the backdrop of an already existing socioeconomic infrastructure.

Moreover, fundamental change takes time. Often the first manifestations of a new technology are worse than the advanced versions of outdated ones. For example, the first fully fledged steam locomotive, the Puffing Devil, was tested in 1801. It was 24 years before George and Robert Stephenson's Locomotion No. 1 carried passengers for the first time. On its first public journey, the steam locomotive traveled at an average speed of 8 miles per hour, much slower than a horse-drawn carriage. As we know today, the decision not to abandon the new technology of steam-powered transportation was the right one.

ASSET BUSTERS
THIS BUILDING IS GREAT AND WOULD FIT INTO OUR PORTFOLIO.
YOU'RE RIGHT. LET'S TOKENIZE IT!
ALMOST DONE! NOW, LET'S GO AND DEFINE THE TOKEN ECONOMY! WE SELL THE TOKENS AT THE MARKET!
DO YOU THINK THERE ARE POTENTIAL BUYERS?
100 U.S. DOLLAR FOR A PART OF THE HISTORICAL CITY HALL!
YOU'RE SELLING RUBBISH!
SCAMMERS!
ARE TOKENS LEGALLY ENFORCEABLE?
YES, THERE ARE NEW LAWS FOR THIS, LIKE THE LIECHTENSTEIN BLOCKCHAIN ACT. IT ALLOWS TOKENIZATION OF ALL KIND OF ASSETS AND RIGHTS WITH LEGAL CERTAINTY!

And so, 10 years on, begun as nothing more than the written word, first on paper and then in code, Bitcoin stands as proof of the pen's omnipotence, and of my early naiveté on the topic of its sharper counterpart. With luck and persistence, or perhaps inevitably, we may here seize upon this phenomenon and emerge – all of us – from one further delusion, from one of the darkest caves through which man has struggled.

Erik Voorhees, CEO ShapeShift

27. Trust and Secession

Bitcoin, Ethereum and other cryptoassets form, as we saw in the last chapter, a new institutional trust structure. Like glue, trust holds a society together. So far, it has mainly been supported by traditional institutions such as nation states and bureaucracies, corporations and banks, the embodiments of "modern" capitalism. They are a creation of the 19th century and have paved the way for humanity to modernity. This was accompanied by the "bourgeoisization" of the world, as the German historian Heinz Köller called this development. The clan structures of feudal states were replaced by hierarchical-centralist institutions of the nation states. As we have seen, they caused an explosion of prosperity unique in history.

But the history of these hierarchical-centralist structures also shows overstretching. Above all, the two World Wars destroyed confidence. After reconstruction—of both the infrastructure and confidence—the Great Moderation began in the early 1980s, a period of low volatility and reasonably stable economic cycles. The majority of the world was in order, and since the collapse of the Eastern Bloc, the end of history seemed to have been reached, as the political scientist Francis Fukuyama wrote in his 1992 book of the same title.

But then came the terrorist attacks of September 11, 2001, and the financial crisis of 2008. Both events shattered confidence in contemporary institutions. More than 10 years after the collapse of Lehman Brothers, it can be said that this confidence is far from restored. On the contrary, institutions are often perceived as powerless, which does not nurture trust but mistrust.

It is no coincidence that Bitcoin was born at the height of the financial crisis (more on this in chapter 1). The cryptocurrency is the antithesis to the existing financial order. It was deliberately not embedded in the existing structures or based on their parameters.

Many people still hold on to existing structures out of fear or uncertainty. And even if they express displeasure, it doesn't mean that they will walk the talk—a loss of trust does not necessarily manifest itself in reality or does so only after a considerable delay. An example of this is the frequently expressed critique of capitalism. Although the numerous problems of today's economic system are obvious, at the same time there is a lack of critical mass to initiate change, because most people understand that we owe our prosperity to what is called a market economy today.

Nevertheless, it cannot be denied that traditional institutions are reaching their limits. They can no longer get out of the zero-interest trap that central banks entered after 2008 to keep financial markets, the real economy and thus society running smoothly. The stability of the financial system is increasingly being called into question. Today, states, companies and households are more heavily indebted than ever before, and the influence of central banks has never been greater. The state of emergency declared by central banks over a decade ago continues unabated, and the exception is becoming the rule.

The two economists Karl Marx and Joseph Schumpeter have already predicted that this would happen—the development is inherent to the system, so to speak. For the economy and society to master the numerous challenges of industrialization, complex organizations such as corporations and state bureaucracies have been indispensable (more on this in chapter 26). However, the price of ever larger companies and growing bureaucracy is the paralyzation and encrustation of structures, and the death of entrepreneurial incentives to innovate.

Economic complexity inevitably leads to political complexity. And it basically outgrows more and more people, which reinforces the impression that political change has come to a standstill. Indeed, states and corporations have functioned largely unchanged for decades—progress thanks to digitization aside. People who want to achieve change are running out of steam with their efforts. This uncertainty and dissatisfaction are also behind the climate demonstrations, which are finally trying to get institutions to adopt strict and uniform climate protection measures.

In addition, political institutions of nation states do not seem to be made for an increasingly global, digital and therefore mobile world. For example, today's understanding of work dates back to the Industrial Age. In a global, digital and mobile world, however, the word *workplace* alone indicates a contradiction. Work should no longer be understood as "staying in one place," but as a non-stationary creative process that is increasingly of a service nature and therefore primarily of an intellectual nature.

From today's perspective, an anachronistic understanding of work is accompanied by antiquated hopes of the welfare state, which also has its roots in the 19th century and is considered an unprecedented achievement. Nevertheless, a change in demographics is increasingly revealing the cracks, especially in pension systems. Younger people, in particular, are losing the confidence that they will one day be able to profit from pension systems. Yet, on the other hand, if they invest some of their savings in bitcoin, they reap a slanted look.

But this would not be a bad strategy given the prospects offered by conventional pension plans. Yield purchasing power, as U.S. economist Keith Weiner calls it, is practically zero today. The concept describes the amount of goods that can be bought with the interest earned on your savings—not much at zero or even negative interest rates.

Making a living from interest rates or even building up capital as in the past is no longer possible today. In order to maintain an adequate standard of living, capital must therefore be consumed. Consequently, pension systems are increasingly cross-subsidized—which also happens at the expense of young people and further undermines their confidence in the future. But capital consumption cannot go on indefinitely.

Interestingly, not all established institutions are equally affected by the loss of confidence. For decades, system-critical economists have argued that the creation of money and the resulting steady increase in debt must at some point come to an abrupt end. But the opposite seems to be the case—the debt carousel continues to spin. In contrast to other government institutions, such as political parties, authorities or even democracy, finance ministries and their main instrument, the government bond, are still fully trusted by investors. Despite massive indebtedness, which in some cases exceeds the value added of the particular government, there are hardly any signs that investors will withdraw confidence from Western treasuries in the foreseeable future. On the contrary, when the financial markets become turbulent, investors flee to U.S. government bonds and other government securities.

This discrepancy is probably related to the fact that the immediate financial benefits of government bonds are more tangible and more constant than, for example, those that people gain through democracy. Even central banks as buyers of last resort continue to enjoy a high level of trust and prestige among the population.

Nevertheless, we should beware of the turkey illusion. Just because the turkey has been fed for 99 days in a row—each feeding confirming its belief that it will be fed every day—doesn't mean it will receive a feeding on the 100th day, Thanksgiving Day. Just when the bird's confidence is at the highest that it will be fed, it is slaughtered instead. In the same way, confidence in the central banks could be tipped over from one day to the next.

Such a loss of confidence would be problematic above all because there have never before been such large sums at stake—in the event of a failure, the global financial system would collapse. Even if some people do not want to admit it, today's highly advanced society, with all its subsidies, grants and endowments, is more dependent on the system's public-private money creation than we suspect, let alone experience, in everyday life. So far central banks prove to be capable of maintaining confidence in the financial system and the various traditional institutions that are built upon it. However, for all the system's apparent functionality, today's institutionalized public-private money creation creates cyclical corrections that affect people differently and in various ways.

This confirms once again that our socioeconomic system is chaotic. Even if politicians, central bankers and business leaders are convinced that they have it under control, on a fundamental level they do not. Because chaotic systems are not deterministic and therefore never completely controllable, stability always increases instability. This is reflected not least in the declining marginal productivity of debt. At the political level, this financial pressure seems to lead to a situation in which all possible adjusting screws must be turned more and more so that the financial engine and thus the economy do not come to a standstill.

At times, these constraints also set new levers in motion in the private sector. For example, Facebook's currency Libra (more on this in chapter 11) announced in June 2019 can also be seen as an attempt to keep the debt-based monetary system functioning. Since Libra is primarily aimed at developing and emerging countries, people's savings would be channeled into the debt securities of the first-world countries. Those who buy Libra would do so with their national fiat currency, and Facebook would then invest the proceeds as a reserve in securities with low volatility (i.e., government bonds). In this way, new funds would flow into our Western monetary system to keep its engine, the debt, running.

With Libra, Facebook shows something else: that the paper money age is slowly but surely coming to an end—and with it the territorial nation state. With the internet, the nation states have already lost sole control over the flow of information. Bitcoin and other cryptoassets are making sure that they also lose control over the transfer of value.

With digitization, capital has become increasingly mobile. Money is already being stored in offshore accounts, often bypassing government treasuries. In addition, value creation is increasingly independent of location and therefore country, and profits can be sent around the globe in a matter of seconds, making taxation even more difficult.

And finally, the crypto world is creating new loopholes that prevent states from levying taxes, and thus maintain the credibility of their debt promises in the long term. The principle of the territorial tax state, according to which taxed income and wealth should be predominantly immobile, seems to be paying off less and less.

New laws that tax at the source of value creation are likely to result in the foreseeable future. Other nation states, on the other hand, could potentially try to tax the immovable connecting factors more heavily. This could drive even more people to capital flight and thus into alternative crypto networks. The new non-central world offers a refuge to all those who do not feel that they are being treated fairly and who want to leave in the sense of "systems competition." One key term that is repeatedly mentioned is "crypto secession."

Nations on the Blockchain

While political secession, as the example of Catalonia shows, can hardly be carried to fruition, the situation with crypto secession is different. It is open to everyone and can take place without people having to leave their nation states or their accustomed environments. One can, for example, work as a blockchain programmer and draw their salary entirely in cryptocurrency. Online services can now be used to buy a number of consumer goods without having to use government fiat money. And if bitcoin and other cryptocurrencies. are not accepted, you can turn to online services that, for example, can find someone to pay the rent for you in exchange for bitcoin. Crypto-anarchists even go so far as to completely renounce a permanent residence to become digital nomads. As perpetual travelers, they cannot be assigned a fixed place of residence and therefore—with the exception of the VAT—cannot really be taxed.

Crypto secession does not mean that you have to say goodbye completely to the traditional world. On the contrary, it gives you the freedom to decide. If you want, you can live with one foot in the centralistic world and with the other in the non-central world—for example, work a conventional job and pay tax on the income earned from it, but at the same time have a second, hidden income that is paid out in bitcoin or an anonymous cryptocurrency (more on this in chapter 29).

However, crypto networks do not offer only earning opportunities away from corporations, traditional workplaces and tax offices. Today, it is also possible to make provisions for one's own future far away from welfare state institutions. Whether it's a simple bitcoin investment, or the attempt to generate a basic income on the blockchain, or dividend income from shares in a blockchain-based casino, or retirement provisions via a fully automatic, smart-contract-based savings plan—the crypto world is bursting with options and experiments.

One of the most ambitious projects is Bitnation. This virtual, cross-border nation wants to establish a blockchain-based self-administration or, as the project itself advertises, "a toolbox for do-it-yourself governance." Bitnation is developing a comprehensive range of services traditionally offered by governments, including a cryptographically secure identification system, blockchain dispute resolution, civil registries, land registers, schools, insurance, security, diplomacy and much more. By its own account, Bitnation has had approximately 15,000 virtual citizens since 2018.

Of course, we are at the beginning of this development. Only with time will it become clear which crypto networks and services will establish themselves as alternatives to conventional institutions. Furthermore, the sword of Damocles of crypto secession should encourage states to cater to the preferences of their citizens. Otherwise—the analog and digital worlds function remarkably similarly in this respect—the dissatisfied will simply emigrate.

CATCHING THE WAVE
A NEW WAVE ON THE HORIZON, THAT ONLY ATTRACTS THE MOST COURAGEOUS AND INNOVATIVE
I NEED TO CATCH THIS WAVE! IT'S JUST WHAT I'VE BEEN WAITING FOR!
...AND ARE LAUGHED AT BY MANY
JACK, THIS WAVE WILL BE SHORT LIVED!
IT'S JUST A BRIEF UPHEAVAL!
DIDN'T I TELL YOU?
...AND THEN ONLY TO JOIN!
HEY "ZUCK", JUST A SHORT UPHEAVAL?
I CAN'T LET YOU HAVE ALL THE FUN ALONE!
HAHA!

The decentralized crypto world is a completely new world. It follows different principles, challenges you intellectually and offers a multitude of new possibilities as an alternative to the traditional world.

Eva, Comic Figure

28. Self-Sovereign Identity in the Blockchain Age

Who am I? In today's world you can't get far without identity. It is attested by a legitimate and verified identity card—you only realize how important it is if you don't carry it with you at a police checkpoint, the bank or a check-in counter at the airport. Even more devastating is the situation in which someone cannot credibly prove their identity. If you do not have a certified identity, economic interaction and social and political participation are hardly possible.

In order for someone's economic, social or political promise to have any chance of validity and acceptance at all, the promisor must verify their identity. This is the only way to guarantee that the promise can be kept. Contractual agreements are never made without prior identification of the contracting parties. At present, it is the traditional institutions mentioned in the previous chapters that identify market players and thus create trust. A relevant example is banks that mediate credit transactions between parties. They guarantee that market participants are aware of each other's identities and can trust each other. Trust creates incentives to enter into contractual agreements.

As our lives became more complex, society came up with various "identity-creating" technologies, which can be used to build a reputation that is linked to identity and thus permits market transactions. In addition to ID cards, there are also brand logos or brand names that reduce the asymmetry of information between people. But in creating and providing the identification that is so important for human interaction, the following question arises: Would a (market) society also be able to create instruments of identification from within itself without the state?

In earlier epochs, first names were sufficient to identify the members of individual clans. Since first names could be attributed to several people even in the narrowest circle, descriptive second names were added, which were often derived from the profession of the respective person—last names such as Baker, Fisher, Miller and Smith still bear witness to this today.

The increasing complexity of our world ultimately necessitated the institutionalization of permanent identities. This took place in the course of the expansion of the fiscal and administrative powers of the state. The previously unbound second names became official family names, and thus permanent and hereditary, even if they no longer coincided with profession. Consequently, state identity became the basis for any form of identification.

The internet age also marks the rise of online identities. Today, these are stored in central data centers operated by Google, Facebook or Microsoft and can be used on the internet for carrying out various transactions. Just as the state manages our "analog" identities, the online giants manage the personal data of their users. However, the ordinary user is no longer just a consumer but the actual product: by using what are usually free services, one feeds companies with data, which they in turn process and monetize. It is no coincidence that the data tech giants are among the financially strongest companies in the world.

Users are not only deprived by the platforms of the added value their data provides, but they are also unable to determine how their data is used and by whom. Just as the bankruptcy of Lehman Brothers ushered in the financial crisis of 2008, revelations about the data analysis firm Cambridge Analytica and its influence on the U.S. election campaign ushered in what can be called the data crisis of 2018. Nothing less than freedom and democracy is at stake.

In order to get the data crisis under control, the EU issued new data protection guidelines in May 2018. The General Data Protection Regulation (GDPR) is intended to allow users to find out at any time how a company uses their data. But loopholes and back doors can always be found—there have been many directives announced before GDPR that turned out only to be tame paper tigers.

A sustainable and genuine solution to the data dilemma could give rise to the concept of self-sovereign identity. Given that we are increasingly part of a global civil society and that we will interact more and more in digital networks in the days to come, such a self-governing identity seems overdue. In the future, responsibility for and control over one's own digital personality will lie with the internet user himself. Just as a person has control over one's own self in the physical world, the same should apply to the digital self. As users, we will one day determine what digital information we make available about ourselves and with whom we want to share it.

There is still no universal identity layer on the internet. In order to be able to identify oneself, a user must remember a wealth of passwords and access codes. As an alternative, tech companies offer the option of logging in with a Facebook or Google profile, for example. Identification inevitably takes place via the respective third party, which in this way collects further data about the user.

With a self-sufficient identity, one would no longer be dependent on identification by third parties. Relevant identity data would be stored on the respective person's device, such as a mobile phone, for example. It is also possible to use so-called identity hubs, which serve to store and transmit data. However, the operators of such hubs would not have the access keys to decrypt the cryptographically secured user data. In addition, users could independently extract the encrypted data at any time.

Only through the interaction of different technologies can self-governing identities become reality. Public blockchains are an important part of the puzzle because they provide a non-central identification management system. So-called "digital identifiers" play a decisive role here, and it will one day be possible to assign them directly to respective users. The identifiers can then be controlled independently via public blockchains. Using Decentralized Identification Documents (DIDs), essentially decentralized identity cards or IDs, users can identify themselves at any time without having to rely on a centralized authority.

DIDs can be registered directly on a public blockchain. Unlike in the transmission of value units such as bitcoin, decentralized identifiers are not subject to the double-spend problem. Ultimately, all that is needed is flawless chronology that is ensured by time stamps on the public blockchain, which acts as an anchor of trust. Metadata adjustments for an identity can be made using an additional protocol. Microsoft, of all companies, has created such an open-source second-layer protocol, called ION, which is comparable to the Lightning Network.

DIDs are user-generated, self-managed and uniquely identifiable—worldwide. This makes them tamper-proof, resistant to censorship and virtually unchangeable. Theoretically, a new DID can be created for each digital interaction, and a pair of DIDs can be generated whenever an internet user contacts another internet user. The goal, however, is for end users to always retain control over their own DIDs and for DIDs to always be based on the data entrusted to the wallet or another identity management application.

In a world where anyone can create an account and any number of DIDs, the question inevitably arises: How can we make sure that a DID-based identity has any value at all, that the real person it claims to represent is really behind it? A DID begins as an empty envelope that is gradually filled with data. This is done one by one through various self-made entries, but also by other users, such as companies, educational institutions and even governments, by issuing attestations to the DID. The more verification and testimonies a DID receives from trustworthy entities, the more trustworthy the decentralized identity itself becomes.

Newer concepts known as social proof systems are trying to make it possible for people to have their DIDs certified by all sorts of close peers in a peer-to-peer manner. Such ideas are still in their infancy but are considered promising because they would not depend on large central entities but could use the decentralized network of one's own peers.

Turn Data into Money

Digital identities nourish the hope that it will no longer be only the large corporations that profit from user data, but that each and every individual user will have the ability to turn their own data into money. Since people exclusively control their own data with self-sufficient identities, they should be able to share it independently with interested customers from the field of digital marketing via the public blockchain and marketplaces based on it to earn money.

But are monetary incentives enough to sell one's own data? Based on the figures available today and conservative assumptions, model calculations show that a Western user could get a couple hundred dollars a year out of their data. That's not much. Nevertheless, many people are excited about the prospects. There are already thoughts that a small basic income might even one day be achieved with self-sovereign digital identities. But in contrast to conventional political attempts and proposals to instate a universal basic income, digital identities and the monetization of one's own data may be able to fulfill the financing of such an income in a much more self-sustaining way. However, there are concerns about the monetization of personal data. Don't data companies earn money with their users' information precisely because they process and refine the data and thus create added value? Don't our data only become valuable when they are aggregated—keyword being *big data*?

A few years ago, researchers at the University of Cambridge and Stanford University found in a study that a computer could predict a subject's personality more accurately than a work colleague by analyzing only 10 Facebook "likes," and even better than a spouse with 300 likes. At some point, this kind of AI (and thus Facebook) could know you even better than you know yourself. So it's quite possible that the social network is in a better position to monetize our data and thus our identities.

Total Surveillance

States might not necessarily welcome the advent of sovereign identity for their citizens. Such an identity would enable greater protection of the private sphere and at the same time call into question existing identity institutions.

The existence of several legal entities should enable people to operate in the cryptoeconomy of the emerging non-central world. As we have seen in the previous chapter, the income generated here could easily be hidden from tax authorities. But the opposite is also conceivable: progressive digitalization could also make it easier to monitor internet participants. Because capital is getting ever more mobile, incentives for further surveillance become greater as well.

China is providing a blueprint of how this could work. In the People's Republic, people are shadowed every step of the way by facial recognition and rewarded or punished for their actions through a social credit system controlled by a centralist hand. It is no coincidence that its development has been accompanied by the gradual abolition of cash. China is systematically and quickly withdrawing paper money and coins from circulation. Mobile payments already amount to more than $16 trillion USD annually—more than 100 times as much as in the U.S. Only 15 percent of transactions are now processed in cash. Tencent's WeChat Pay and Alibaba's Alipay are the dominant digital payment systems in China. Together they have a market share of 92 percent.

Of course, the counterargument is that in democratic Western countries, such a complete surveillance of citizens is unimaginable. But a large part of the techno-panoptic system used in China was developed in the West—and was already in use, as Edward Snowden revealed in 2013. The former NSA employee published thousands of top-secret documents about U.S. government surveillance programs and their allies. According to them, governments even paid private companies to obtain information about certain citizens. Nevertheless, the next and final chapter sets out to show that privacy is still not dead.

SHOWTIME!
ST. MORITZ, SWITZERLAND
THE ENTIRE WHO-IS-WHO OF THE CRYPTO WORLD HAS GATHERED IN THE SWISS ALPS FOR THE YEARLY CRYPTO CONGRESS. THE MOST IMPORTANT PURPOSE: SHOWING TO THE WORLD THE CONCEPT BEHIND BLOCKCHAIN AND BITCOIN.
YOU'RE FINALLY HERE! EVERYTHING IS PREPARED. TODAY, WE'LL SHOW THE WCFG WHAT THE FUTURE IS ALL ABOUT.
LONG BITCOIN, SHORT THE WCFG BANKERS!
ARE YOU READY?!
YOU BET!
SHOWDOWN!
THIS IS IT! LET'S GO IN!

If we do not value our privacy today, and do not put into place mechanisms to protect, preserve, and enhance our privacy using technology, then we create the conditions for a future where our privacy has no value, and cannot be protected, preserved, or enhanced.

Meltem Demirors, CSO CoinShares

29. Man's Most Precious Good

Due to global digital networking, surveillance seems absolute. For many, privacy today is only a memory of days long past. Anyone who wants to achieve at least a semblance of it must retreat into the woods and largely do without digital devices. Or, as paradoxical as it may sound, immerse oneself completely in the digital world—in the future, this will probably be the last refuge for privacy. Asymmetric cryptography (see chapter 24) makes it possible for things to remain private, even if they are stored on public, freely accessible blockchains. As far as financial privacy in cyberspace is concerned, bitcoin as digital cash opened the door to it quite wide (see chapter 1).

In economic commerce, cash guarantees the ability to act and stay sovereign. It offers the very ability to make decisions independently. It is the ability to try things out in one's own way, to be successful and rewarded, or to make mistakes, fail and learn from them. Without a form of cash, there can be no fully open society, since eliminating cash means that all transactions are necessarily dependent on third parties, undermining financial privacy and sovereignty. Of course, one cannot deny that privacy can also be misused for disreputable or reprehensible purposes—for example, on the very darkest shops on the dark web.

The internet can be roughly divided into three areas. When we read the news, stream films on Netflix or shop at Amazon, we use the "surface web." Below this is the "deep web." These are pages that lie behind a registration or payment barrier and are therefore not found by search engines. The third level is the dark web, or Darknet, which is not accessed via ordinary browsers but through a special one. The best-known of these browsers is "Tor," which is an abbreviation for "The Onion Router." Therefore Darknet websites end with the extension ".onion."

The fact that you can use the dark web anonymously is due to onion routing. With this anonymization technique, the Tor browser does not connect directly to the website being accessed, but instead establishes a randomly chosen connection route with several proxies (i.e., intermediate stations) between the initial computer and the end server.

These proxies are scattered all over the world. If you want to access a specific page from Switzerland via the Tor browser, you first need to connect to a proxy in Ukraine, for example. Then jump to another proxy in Guatemala before a new connection is established with an intermediate station in Israel. Only the last proxy transmits the request to the end server. This connection is reestablished approximately every 10 minutes.

In addition, the individual data packets within the Tor network are always transmitted in encrypted form. The Tor browser uses end-to-end encryption for this purpose. In this way, it conceals the origin of the data. Only the exit proxy passes the packet on to the end server in unencrypted form under certain circumstances. This multilayered connection method using different proxies also explains the Tor name and logo: it is an onion with several layers.

In addition to black-market and file-sharing sites on which drugs, weapons, pirated copies or illegal pornography are offered for sale, the dark web also has many constructive websites: uncensored media channels, contact points for whistleblowers and forums on all kinds of topics. Of the approximately 40,000 Tor hidden services, or "onion services," not all are illegal. According to estimates, about 70 percent of Tor users are journalists, bloggers and opposition politicians from repressive states.

To this day Bitcoin is used used as a means of payment on the Darknet, which is mainly due to the fact that the cryptocurrency offers non-intermediated payment option. Although no one can censor a payment, transactions are still traceable. This is mainly due to the fact that Bitcoin is not anonymous but pseudonymous. This means that it is not possible to find out who owns which bitcoin and who carries out which transaction simply by looking at the Bitcoin network since wallet addresses and transactions consist of arbitrary number-and-letter codes (the often mentioned hash). This hash pseudonymizes the wallet and transaction address; the real user behind it cannot be determined without further clues. However, if a person had to identify himself during the installation of his wallet, the hash address is linked to his real identity. Once a hash address can be assigned to a person, all of their transactions can be traced since they are publicly viewable by everyone via the decentralized ledger. This allows government agencies, analysts and other interested parties to fully investigate the Bitcoin network by linking Bitcoin addresses to IP addresses or other identifying information.

Companies such as Chainalysis are already using various analysis methods to evaluate transactions and check for fraud, money laundering and other inconsistencies. In this way, state internet investigators in particular are said to have succeeded several times in arresting offenders in connection to drugs, child pornography and other crimes.

In the course of such blockchain analyses, so-called tainted coins (i.e., contaminated bitcoin) are also identified, which then have to be branded by exchanges. These are, for example, coins from money laundering or other illegal businesses, or tokens that are associated with an unwelcome party or person such as Hezbollah or Kim Jong-Un from North Korea. In this way, these bitcoin lose their attractiveness because they are no longer accepted in transactions or are accepted only at a discount.

Some see this as one of the greatest dangers for Bitcoin, since the cryptoasset could lose its fungibility, or interchangeability (see chapter 25), as a result of such measures. The fact that each bitcoin can be exchanged one-to-one for another bitcoin is essential for its liquidity. If too many coins can only be exchanged at a discount or cannot be traded at all, this leads to friction costs that undermine the function of bitcoin as a medium of exchange.

Anonymous Cryptocurrencies

Despite its pseudonymity Bitcoin is still the main cryptocurrency used on the Darknet. This seems rather surprising given that there are so-called privacy coins, which, as suggested by their name, grant users much more anonymity. While Bitcoin has a public ledger that makes real transactions and ownership transparent, privacy coins conceal this information. The most important representatives of this category are Monero and Zcash. Monero is the privacy coin with the highest market capitalization, and privacy is anchored at the level of its basic protocol. It uses a feature called ring confidential transactions (RingCT) for this purpose.

Many additional coins, also known as decoys, are added to each transaction—this combination is called the RingCT. This way, coins are mixed together so that outside observers cannot tell whether the original coins or decoys have been issued. Ring signatures can be used to mix up different transactions and cover them up. In addition, the respective payment amounts can be concealed within the framework of confidential transactions. A cryptographic trick ensures that the mathematics are correct in the end. Nevertheless, only the sender and recipient of a transaction know how many coins have changed hands.

Alongside Monero, Zcash has established itself as the second-largest privacy coin, but it works somewhat differently. Zcash has two different types of addresses. T-addresses are publicly accessible. If you use Zcash and a t-address, you are not anonymous but pseudonymous as with Bitcoin. Z-addresses, the second type, are also called shielded addresses, and they are encrypted on the blockchain and therefore not visible. As with Monero, a cryptographic method is used to ensure that the underlying mathematics work without the exact numbers being recognizable. A form of zero-knowledge cryptography called zk-SNARKs (which stands for zero-knowledge succinct noninteractive argument of knowledge) is what enables Zcash users to prove the ownership and validity of certain information without disclosing that data to third parties.

Zero-knowledge proofs allow cryptocurrencies to prove that a transaction is considered valid by the recipient without having to disclose the actual transaction data. This allows the sender, recipient and amount to remain anonymous. Zk-SNARKs are also important in connection with self-sufficient identity and identity verification discussed in the previous chapter. For example, zk-SNARKs can be used to identify a person during an age check—for example, when buying alcohol—without having to reveal the exact age.

Zcash allows a variety of transactions. If, for example, a payment goes from one t-address to several z-addresses, it is not clear where the coins are transferred to. If coins are sent from one z-address to one t-address, it is not possible to see where the coins come from. From a privacy point of view, it becomes really interesting if only z-addresses are involved in a transaction: the entire transaction is then encrypted. In such a shielded transaction, the sender, recipient and the amount sent stay a secret.

However, anyone using z-addresses with Zcash automatically becomes suspected of wanting to hide something. Using t-addresses instead helps users avoid this general suspicion, but this reduces the number of z-addresses used. The less that z-addresses are used instead of t-addresses, the greater the risk that the latter will reveal information about the former. With Monero, every transaction is based on ring signatures and is therefore confidential, which is why this problem occurs less frequently. But because Monero only allows anonymous transactions, anyone who uses it could be viewed as suspicious.

The Thin Line

Bitcoin now also offers several options for anonymizing transactions at the application level. Thanks to Bitcoin mixers or tumblers such as SharedCoin, TumbleBit and CoinJoin, Bitcoin transactions can hardly be traced, and the traces of individual bitcoin units can no longer be found in the network.

Such applications are even integrated into certain bitcoin wallets, such as the Wasabi Wallet and the Samourai Wallet. Essentially, CoinJoin bundles several transactions into one larger transaction in order to hide which bitcoin go from which sender to which receiver. One negative point against mixer services is that many of them are still handled by centralized third parties, so coins could easily be stolen. Non-centralized solutions are being worked on.

Another problem is that CoinJoin is less secure than commonly claimed. Analysis techniques can still be used to expose individual transactions, especially when many transactions with different quantities of bitcoin are collected. This is why there is a CoinJoin option that bundles only transactions of the same amount (0.1 bitcoin, for example) to create homogeneity—making the work much more difficult for snoopers.

With a bit of technical know-how, you can get more privacy within the Bitcoin network these days. Since Bitcoin is pseudonymous by default, the same dynamics are in work here as with Zcash. Those who use anonymizing software for their transactions place themselves under general suspicion. For example, trading exchanges could be forced to reject Bitcoin transactions that come from CoinJoin, which would again damage the fungibility of Bitcoin.

Interestingly, for some time now, Bitcoin has been discussing the implementation of what are called Schnorr signatures. With the SegWit update of 2018 (more about this in chapter 18), an implementation of Schnorr is now theoretically possible. Many cryptographers currently regard Schnorr signatures as the best cryptographic signatures.

Schnorr signatures were invented in the 1980s by Claus-Peter Schnorr, a German cryptographer. However, several patents filed by this former professor at the University of Frankfurt prevented their use for years. The patents expired in 2008. Theoretically, Satoshi Nakamoto could have implemented the Schnorr signature system when he programmed the Bitcoin blockchain. But Schnorr signatures were neither standardized nor widely used at the time, which is why Nakamoto opted for another standard, the Elliptic Curve Digital Signature Algorithm, or ECDSA for short.

Digital signatures are indispensable for verification within the network. Bitcoin is based on public-key cryptography. While the public key is broadcast to the network and represents the recipient's address for receiving bitcoin, the private key is the access key, like a PIN, that can be used to sign Bitcoin transactions and thus show that one is in possession of the corresponding units.

Schnorr signatures will one day inherit the ECDSA standard. Perhaps the biggest advantage they offer is on the level of multisignature (or multisig) Bitcoin transactions, which require more than just one private access key to authorize. For example, a two-of-three multisig address requires two private access keys to authorize a transaction. Only if two of the three designated private keys sign the transaction will its execution really follow. This way, the risks and responsibility of owning bitcoin can be shared among several people.

Using Schnorr signatures, several keys can be aggregated into a single key in a multisig transaction, which then represents all individual keys. Such key aggregations make transactions much more data efficient. Only one signature is required per transaction, regardless of how many sender addresses it contains.

CoinJoin transactions would also benefit from Schnorr signatures—the bitcoin of several senders could be combined in one transaction and signed with a secure key. In this case, the bitcoin units of the individual senders would not be mixed, but would still correspond to the respective users. And they would reach the correct recipients without the transfers being visible from the outside.

The Schnorr signature update would also make CoinJoin transactions cheaper because the transaction fees can be divided between the different sender addresses. This is likely to lead to an increase in number of such Schnorr-based CoinJoin transactions among Bitcoin users, which in turn would increase the anonymous use of Bitcoin.

The Lightning Network (more on this in chapter 19) also contributes to more privacy since its transactions are anonymous. The consequences of a more anonymous Bitcoin network overall, however, are difficult to assess today. If Bitcoin usage should become much more anonymous, it will not be welcomed warmly by folks having to implement know-your-customer (KYC) and anti-money laundering (AML) regulations and could hamper the integration of Bitcoin into everyday business activities and investment portfolios.

It seems inevitable that the debate about privacy will intensify within the communities of individual public blockchains in the coming years. Bitcoin in particular is still strongly committed to the cypherpunk ethos, of which privacy is an important, if not the most important, pillar. Some Bitcoin cypherpunks also argue for an anonymized Bitcoin base layer, as is the case with Monero and Zcash.

Others argue against it because they consider the ledger's publicness to be essential. Only if the Bitcoin ledger remains accessible to all parties can everyone ensure that no secret inflation of the cryptocurrency takes place. In September 2018, a so-called inflation bug was discovered within the Bitcoin source code. Fortunately, it was fixed before anyone could take advantage of it. But an essential lesson was learned from this incident: not even the Bitcoin code is infallible. It is therefore all the more important that the code, the Bitcoin blockchain and thus the entire transaction history remain publicly accessible in the future.

CONTINUED...

STOP!
YOUR CRYPTO NONSENSE WILL END HERE!
LORD IB VON KRATZ!
YOU THINK YOU CAN INTIMIDATE US WITH THIS?
COOL IT WITH THE GUNS? THIS IS TAKING IT TOO FAR!
NOBODY MOVES!
WE'LL SOLVE THIS PEACEFULLY! JUST SURRENDER NOW!

CONTINUED...

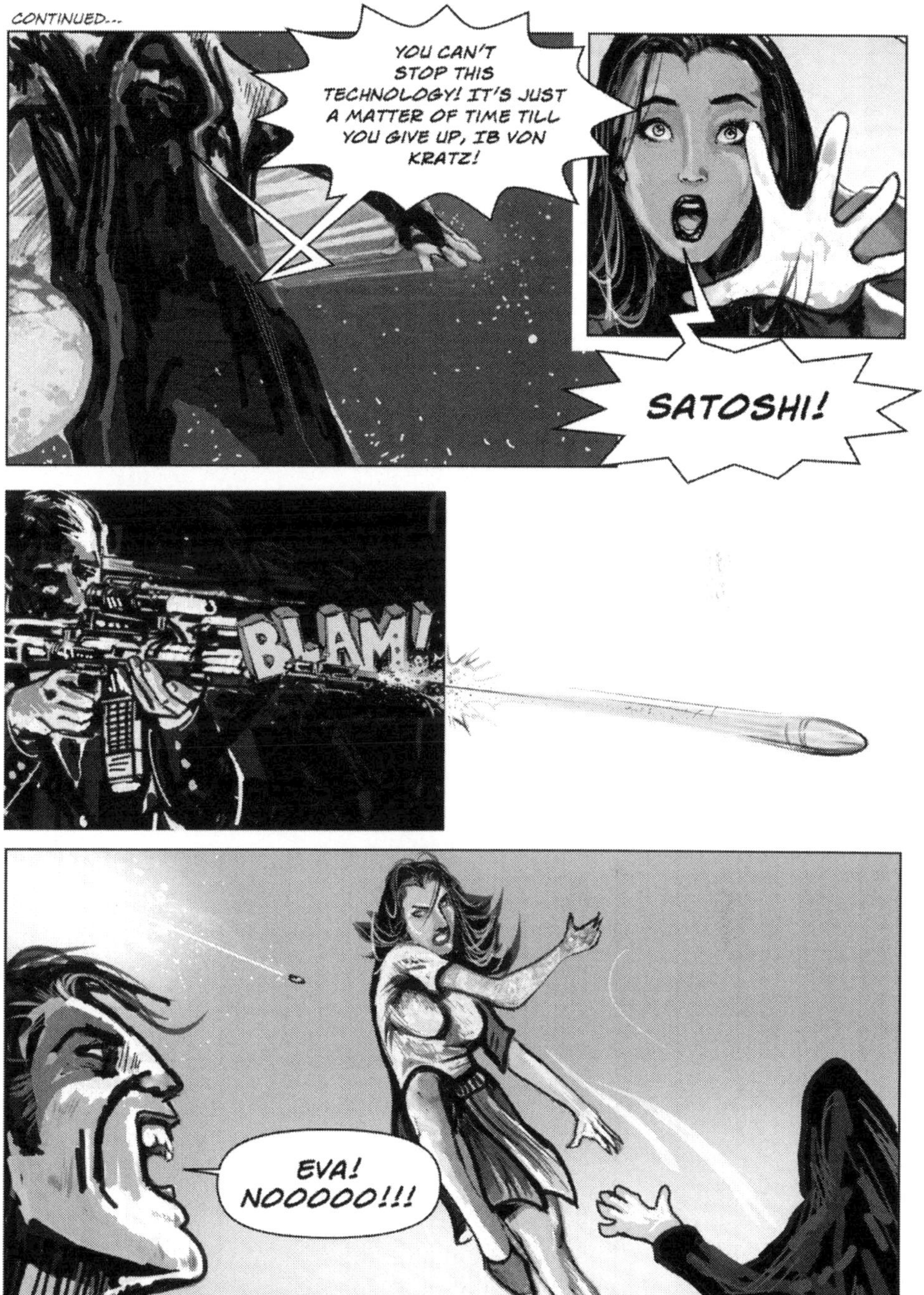
YOU CAN'T STOP THIS TECHNOLOGY! IT'S JUST A MATTER OF TIME TILL YOU GIVE UP, IB VON KRATZ!
SATOSHI!
BLAM!
EVA! NOOOOO!!!

Closing Words

Primacy of the Digital

Our journey through the new non-central world of crypto is coming to an end. I would like to conclude with an objection that I often hear when I talk to people about cryptoassets: in contrast to physical, analog things, Bitcoin and similar assets are completely virtual and digital, and therefore neither tangible nor graspable, and would thus lack any real basis of value.

The juxtaposition of analog and digital seems obvious at first glance. However, it is important to recognize that it is based on a way of thinking that is increasingly losing its validity. For more and more people, the digital has become a matter that is taken for granted. While older generations may still make excursions into digital spheres as "tourists" of an analog world, Gen Z, millennials and even the slightly older Generation X have long been at home in a digital world where bits dominate atoms.

Having grown up mostly as digital natives, they cultivate a digital lifestyle from the ground up. This gives them a completely different attitude toward the digital than people who have been socialized knowing only the analog world. One of the most impressive examples of this development is the video game *Fortnite*. For so-called Google kids, *Fortnite* is much more than a video game—it is the reality of their lives in which they socialize and spend more time than in the "real" world.

February 2019 was the biggest moment in *Fortnite*'s young history: the American electronic music producer DJ Marshmello gave an in-game concert. His performance took place completely virtually on a show stage within the computer game. *Fortnite* players could participate only as their virtual avatars. And that's what they did: almost 11 million mostly young people danced as their game characters in the digital concert.

Such events may seem surreal and curious to older generations, but for the majority of Google kids, they are completely normal. Just as V-Bucks, the currency within *Fortnite*, are a valuable asset for them. From this famous in-game currency, it is only a small step to Bitcoin and other cryptocurrencies (more on this in chapter 26).

This digital mindset also explains why some female millennials may be just as happy to receive a digital bouquet of flowers on their smartphones on

Valentine's Day as they are to receive roses that have grown in the soil. Digital gold could seem more real to this generation than real precious metal.

As a species, we are in the process of digitizing our reality. This is probably just another iteration, not the last, of a cultivation process that humanity has been going through since time immemorial. We learn to think in gradually more abstract categories and tap into new potentials again and again. The process of cultural adaptation to fully adopt digital values has only just begun.

Therefore, it makes less and less sense to perceive the virtual and physical worlds as separate spheres of human trade. They are in the process of increasingly merging with each other and finally becoming one.

The fact that digital bits are suddenly on the same level as physical atoms is initially somewhat uncanny. A look at the deepfake phenomenon is worthwhile as an example. This is a term that has been in common use since 2017 for the technology used to create deceptively authentic images and videos. Many politicians, actors and other celebrities have already fallen victim to this practice. Deepfake videos put words into their mouths that they never said, or made them perform actions they never did. What is real and what is not?

The digital is increasingly blurring our notions of reality and what is genuine. We are simply not used to a world in which digital information dominates. Interestingly, even in the case of deepfake technology, public blockchains could help distinguish real from false. As an unchangeable and non-manipulable database, they create the possibility of chronologically anchoring data and thus proving that a video, for example, was created at an illogical time and must therefore be fake.

Those who continue to ignore the crypto world and its endless possibilities do so at their own risk.

References

1. Bitcoin and Its Beginnings
Bitcoin and Cash:
https://medium.com/@hasufly/bitcoin-is-a-hedge-against-the-cashless-society-e98b5d8c68cc
Bitcoin and The Byzantine Generals Problem:
https://www.youtube.com/watch?v=SF362xxcfdk
Difference between Decentralization and Non-Centralism:
https://www.libinst.ch/publikationen/LI-Paper-Nef-Non-Zentralismus-d.pdf

2. An Evolutionary Counterrevolution
Bitcoin & Wikileaks:
https://medium.com/@petershin45/hate-bitcoin-this-might-change-your-mind-837963c24d70
Hayek & Knowledge:
https://object.cato.org/sites/cato.org/files/articles/hayek-use-knowledge-society.pdf
Social Scalability:
https://unenumerated.blogspot.com/2017/02/money-blockchains-and-social-scalability.html
Triple Entry Accounting:
https://medium.com/coinmonks/why-bitcoins-lightning-network-is-the-ingenious-10dc1ad9ccae

3. Money or Gold?
Bitcoin and Mises' Regression Theorem:
https://nakamotoinstitute.org/static/docs/origins-of-bitcoin.pdf
Hayek and Denationalization of Money:
https://nakamotoinstitute.org/static/docs/denationalisation.pdf
Bitcoin & Time:
https://anchor.fm/tales-from-the-crypt/episodes/Tales-from-the-Crypt-60-Misir-Mahmudov-e3aibh
Bitcoin versus Gold:
https://www.goldmoney.com/research/goldmoney-insights/drop-gold-and-the-myths-we-re-told
Digital Money and Digital Gold:
https://medium.com/@tuurdemeester/bitcoin-digital-gold-or-digital-cash-both-382a346e6c79
Antifragility:
https://www.artofmanliness.com/articles/beyond-sissy-resilience-on-becoming-antifragile/

Lindy Effect:
https://medium.com/shakepay/why-the-lindy-effect-predicts-that-bitcoin-will-last-aa6b3a89229a
Bitcoin and Magic:
http://www.konradsgraf.com/blog1/2014/9/19/bitcoin-magic-fraud-or-sufficiently-advanced-technology.html

4. To the Brave the World Belongs!
Bitcoin is fractal:
https://www.forbes.com/sites/investor/2019/01/23/bitcoin-is-fractal/
Bitcoin and Valuation:
https://medium.com/@adamant_capital/a-primer-on-bitcoin-investor-sentiment-and-changes-in-saving-behavior-a5fb70109d32

5. Welcome to the World of Finance
Bitcoin and Fractional Reserve Banking
https://medium.com/@whatbitcoindid/the-threat-of-fractional-reserve-bitcoin-from-wall-street-with-saifedean-ammous-caitlin-long-2d61e63ac868
Blockchain and Wall-Street:
https://www.youtube.com/watch?v=9PAINpC9FVc
Bitcoin and unbacked claims:
https://www.forbes.com/sites/caitlinlong/2018/08/21/two-things-that-dont-mix-well-bitcoin-rehypothecation-and-chain-forks/#14f584281e14
Bitcoin and the Repo Markets:
https://www.forbes.com/sites/caitlinlong/2019/09/25/the-real-story-of-the-repo-market-meltdown-and-what-it-means-for-bitcoin/
Bitcoin and Hodlers:
https://tokeneconomy.co/hodlers-are-the-revolutionaries-66c8362ef9eb

6. Declaring War on Wall-Street
ICO and Capital Markets:
https://www.forbes.com/sites/caitlinlong/2018/07/22/icos-were-45-of-ipos-in-q2-2018-as-cryptos-disrupt-investment-banks/#3b811260794c

7. Made and Designed for Central Banks
Bitcoin and Venezuela:
https://www.longhash.com/news/opinion-no-venezuela-is-not-becoming-a-bitcoin-nation
Central Banks and Digital Currencies:
https://www.economist.com/finance-and-economics/2018/05/26/central-banks-should-consider-offering-accounts-to-everyone

8. From Bitcoin to Stablecoins
MakerDAO:
https://medium.com/makerdao/stablecoins-strengths-weaknesses-62cd47bb7fbf
Three Types of Stablecoins:
https://hackernoon.com/a-comprehensive-guide-to-decentralized-stablecoins-22f66553c807
The Perils of Price Stability:
http://www.permwinterschool.ru/download2019/2_5Sergey_Ivliev_Stablecoins_An_elusive_dream_of_stability.pdf
Stablecoin Trilemma:
https://medium.com/@byrnehobart/the-stablecoin-trilemma-d763ff64a6eb
Hayek and Stablecoins:
https://medium.com/@QwQiao/hayek-and-stablecoins-3c7f3291d728

9. From Bitcoin to Blockchain
Essence of the Blockchain:
https://medium.com/@cayle/so-you-think-you-need-a-blockchain-part-i-a75389808c00
Private and Public Blockchains:
https://medium.com/@rtylersmith/public-and-private-blockchains-enemies-or-allies-45f050c38fc0
Blockchain as a Meaningless Term:
https://medium.com/s/story/blockchain-is-a-semantic-wasteland-9450b6e5012
Permissioned Blockchains:
https://www.multichain.com/blog/category/private-blockchains/

10. To Fork or Not to Fork
Crypto Evolution:
https://blog.ycombinator.com/crypto-evolution/
The Future is Forked:
https://kwokchain.com/2018/05/01/the-future-is-forked/219
Forkology:
https://www.youtube.com/watch?v=rpeceXY1QBM&t=510s
Post-Scarcity Economics:
https://medium.com/@byrnehobart/cryptocurrencies-and-post-post-scarcity-economics-4dfbc04d84c6

11. The Supremacy of Permissionless Innovation
Permissionless Innovation:
https://www.youtube.com/watch?v=a86g-z8bD6g
Bank the Unbanked:
https://medium.com/altcoin-magazine/you-dont-want-to-help-bank-the-unbanked-94e4d6015c53

Libra and the Reserve Fund:
https://twitter.com/CaitlinLong_/status/1140974654812635136

12. The Diverse World of Cryptoassets
Swiss Decentralization and Crypto:
https://www.libertarianism.org/building-tomorrow/crypto-switzerland-matching-decentralized-government-decentralized-currency
Skin-in-the-game-token:
https://medium.com/tbis-weekly-bits/skin-in-the-game-coins-da0afdfdc650

13. The Rise of Ethereum
Vitalik and Ethereum:
https://medium.com/conversations-with-tyler/vitalik-buterin-tyler-cowen-cryptocurrency-blockchain-tech-3a2b20c12c97
Exahash-Era:
https://news.bitcoin.com/the-exahash-era-sha-256-mining-is-a-significant-achievement-in-computer-engineering/
An Overview about Ethereum:
https://www.delphidigital.io/ethereum

14. A New Internet
Blockchain as a Solution for Internet's Original Sin:
https://www.coindesk.com/can-blockchain-save-us-from-the-internets-original-sin/
Web 3.0:
https://medium.com/@ConsenSys/welcome-to-3-0-f4552fb02302
Monetary Layer for the Internet:
https://medium.com/@thibm/a-monetary-layer-for-the-internet-4b6d412e43d4
Decentralized Storage Solution:
https://medium.com/bitfwd/what-is-decentralised-storage-ipfs-filecoin-sia-storj-swarm-5509e476995f

15. Smart Contracts and Their Applications
Smart Contracts and Humans:
https://hackernoon.com/why-smart-contracts-still-need-human-logic-e4c07885e26a
The Promise of Smart Contracts:
https://www.libertarianism.org/columns/promise-smart-contracts
A Critique of Smart Contracts:
https://medium.com/@jimmysong/the-truth-about-smart-contracts-ae825271811f
The Oracle Problem:
https://medium.com/@DelphiSystems/the-oracle-problem-856ccbdbd14f

Google and Oracles:
https://cloud.google.com/blog/products/data-analytics/building-hybrid-blockchain-cloud-applications-with-ethereum-and-google-cloud

16. The World of Decentralized Finance
DeFi Overview:
https://defipulse.com/
DeFi Concepts Explained:
https://bankless.substack.com/archive
Money Legos:
https://medium.com/totle/building-with-money-legos-ab63a58ae764
The Digital Financial Stack:
https://medium.com/pov-crypto/ethereum-the-digital-finance-stack-4ba988c6c14b

17. Beyond the Blockchain
The Future of the Machine Economy:
https://www.youtube.com/watch?v=6mkSVUoND9A
The Mastermind behind Hashgraph:
https://www.youtube.com/watch?v=S2MHCWMQXY8&t=825s

18. Childhood Diseases of a New Technology
Bitcoin and Bicycles:
https://medium.com/embracingparadoxes/quest-for-patience-c397d2ad820d

19. Lightning Fast
Lightning – quo vadis:
https://medium.com/@digitsu/lightning-network-will-it-save-or-break-bitcoin-5c8645924cb6
Where the Lightning Network could go:
https://medium.com/@timevalueofbtc/the-time-value-of-bitcoin-3807b91f02d2
Introduction to Lightning:
https://hackernoon.com/christian-decker-an-introduction-to-the-lightning-network-7041eaa4d0f8
HTTP for Bitcoin:
https://www.youtube.com/watch?v=3PcR4HWJnkY&t=646s
Liquid:
https://www.youtube.com/watch?v=GwnFfp5xIag

20. Conflict of Visions
A Conflict of Crypto Visions:
https://medium.com/@yelmandjraark/a-conflict-of-crypto-visions-160dbfc33bfa

Monetary Policy of Bitcoin:
https://bankless.substack.com/p/btcs-monetary-policy-is-overrated
Monetary Policy of Ethereum:
https://bankless.substack.com/p/eths-monetary-policy-is-underrated
The Visions of Ethereum:
https://tokeneconomy.co/visions-of-ether-590858bf848e
Plasma:
https://medium.com/@argongroup/ethereum-plasma-explained-608720d3c60e
Validators:
https://media.consensys.net/examining-the-proposed-validator-economics-of-ethereum-2-0-82b934fb4326
Sidechains versus State Channels:
https://hackernoon.com/difference-between-sidechains-and-state-channels-2f5dfbd10707
State Channels:
https://www.jeffcoleman.ca/state-channels/
Sharding:
https://github.com/ethereum/wiki/wiki/Sharding-FAQs

21. Disagreeing on Consensus
Non-Centralized Clock:
https://grisha.org/blog/2018/01/23/explaining-proof-of-work/
The Anatomy of Proof-of-Work:
https://bitcointechtalk.com/the-anatomy-of-proof-of-work-98c85b6f6667
Proof-of-Stake:
https://medium.com/@VitalikButerin/a-proof-of-stake-design-philosophy-506585978d51
Critique of Proof-of-Stake:
https://medium.com/@tuurdemeester/critique-of-buterins-a-proof-of-stake-design-philosophy-49fc9ebb36c6
Comparison of Consensus Mechanisms:
https://blog.bitmex.com/complete-guide-to-proof-of-stake-ethereums-latest-proposal-vitalik-buterin-interview
Imporant Distinction between Proof-of-Work and Proof-of-Stake:
https://medium.com/@hugonguyen/work-is-timeless-stake-is-not-554c4450ce18

22. The Burning Energy Question
Bitcoin isn't just green:
https://www.theblockcrypto.com/2019/01/30/bitcoin-doesnt-incentivize-green-energy/
What you need to know about Bitcoin and Energy:
https://hackernoon.com/how-everyones-wrong-about-the-energy-used-in-bitcoin-mining-fe3009fd9102

Proof-of-Work is efficient:
https://blog.picks.co/pow-is-efficient-aa3d442754d3
Bitcoin does not waste Energy:
https://hackernoon.com/bitcoin-doesnt-waste-electricity-649694ea3605
Why Critics of Bitcoin are wrong about its Energy Use:
https://hackernoon.com/the-reports-of-bitcoin-environmental-damage-are-garbage-5a93d32c2d7
Bitcoin Electricity Consumption Index:
http://www.epe.admin.cam.ac.uk/cambridge-bitcoin-electricity-consumption-index-cbeci

23. Blockchain and the Law

Who's to sue:
https://medium.com/forbes/when-blockchains-crash-who-can-you-sue-824b02479f85
Decentralization and the Law:
https://papers.ssrn.com/sol3/papers.cfm?abstract_id=3326244
Property Rights and Bitcoin:
https://medium.com/@hasufly/bitcoin-and-the-promise-of-independent-property-rights-8f10e5c7efa8
The Internet's Magna Charta:
https://medium.com/blockchain-capital-blog/the-internets-magna-carta-moment-bitcoin-the-value-of-strong-assurances-56fb86887b8a
The New Era of Crypto:
https://medium.com/@dergigi/the-magic-dust-of-cryptography-c8ecd79ae13a
Bitcoin and Property:
https://medium.com/blockchain-capital-blog/the-most-interesting-property-in-the-world-22f90a11bb87
Crypto Law:
https://medium.com/@gabriel.j.shapiro/in-defense-of-szabos-law-for-a-mostly-non-legal-crypto-system-8f1ce2b364a6
Bitcoin and Human Rights:
https://medium.com/@alexgladstein/a-human-rights-activists-response-to-bitcoin-critics-d50e6760ee80

24. Cryptoeconomics and Blockchain Governance

Blockchain and Trustlessness:
https://medium.com/@preethikasireddy/eli5-what-do-we-mean-by-blockchains-are-trustless-aa420635d5f6
Byzantine Political Economy:
https://papers.ssrn.com/sol3/papers.cfm?abstract_id=3344110
Institution versus Organization:
https://medium.com/@festina_lente_2/institutions-versus-organizations-95ac29f10ee7

Bitcoins Social Contract:
https://medium.com/@hasufly/bitcoins-social-contract-1f8b05ee24a9 Bitcoin
Hard Assurances:
https://medium.com/@nic__carter/unpacking-bitcoins-assurances-a3c98824d3f0
Bitcoin Governance:
https://medium.com/@pierre_rochard/bitcoin-governance-37e86299470f
Who Controls Bitcoin:
https://medium.com/@lopp/who-controls-bitcoin-core-c55c0af91b8a
Cryptoeconomics:
https://medium.com/l4-media/making-sense-of-cryptoeconomics-c6455776669
Advanced Guide to Cryptoeconomics:
https://hackernoon.com/an-advanced-guide-to-cryptoeconomics-5a998aa97621

25. The Token Economy
The Future of Network Effects:
https://medium.com/public-market/the-future-of-network-effects-tokenization-and-the-end-of-extraction-a0f895639ffb
Non-fungible Tokens:
https://blockonomi.com/non-fungible-tokens/
Tokens:
https://thecontrol.co/tokens-tokens-and-more-tokens-d4b177fbb443
Network Ownership Effect:
http://continuations.com/post/148098927445/crypto-tokens-and-the-coming-age-of-protocol
Tokenization and Artificial Intelligence:
https://blog.modex.tech/tokenization-of-physical-assets-and-the-impact-of-internet-of-things-and-artificial-intelligence-c08cdf8432a4
High-Frequency Barter:
https://papers.ssrn.com/sol3/papers.cfm?abstract_id=3158047
Token Economics:
https://medium.com/ezraneweconomythoughts/what-is-tokenomics-and-which-school-of-economics-would-crush-it-a796f7764273

26. Capitalism after Satoshi
Blockchain and Markets:
https://hackernoon.com/reflections-on-the-best-blockchain-tweets-ever-written-d488af960d4f
How Satoshi changed Capitalism:
https://papers.ssrn.com/sol3/papers.cfm?abstract_id=3299734
Ledgers:
https://papers.ssrn.com/sol3/papers.cfm?abstract_id=3157421

27. Trust and Secession
Nation-States and Blockchain:
https://papers.ssrn.com/sol3/papers.cfm?abstract_id=2709713
Crypto Secession:
https://mesosoupblog.files.wordpress.com/2016/03/cryptosecession-and-the-limitis-of-taxation-towards-a-theory-of-non-territorial-internal-exit-compressed.pdf
The Rise of the Sovereign Individual:
https://medium.com/coinmonks/the-rise-of-the-sovereign-individual-4ac50c82b760

28. Self-Sovereign Identity in the Blockchain Age
Digital Identity:
https://www.bundesblock.de/wp-content/uploads/2019/01/ssi-paper.pdf
Microsoft and Decentralized Identity:
https://query.prod.cms.rt.microsoft.com/cms/api/am/binary/RE2DjfY

29. Man's Most Precious Good
Monero:
https://bitcoinmagazine.com/articles/battle-privacycoins-why-monero-hard-beat-and-hard-scale/
Bitcoin and Privacy:
https://bitcoinmagazine.com/articles/bitcoin-privacycoin-tech-making-bitcoin-more-private/
Zcash:
https://bitcoinmagazine.com/articles/battle-privacycoins-zcash-groundbreaking-if-you-trust-it/
Schnorr-Signatures:
https://medium.com/digitalassetresearch/schnorr-signatures-the-inevitability-of-privacy-in-bitcoin-b2f45a1f7287
Privacy as a Precious Good:
https://medium.com/@Melt_Dem/im-not-an-international-drug-dealer-3e8e3c75c57c
Privacy in the 21 Century:
https://coincenter.org/entry/we-must-protect-our-ability-to-transact-privately-online

About the Authors

Pascal Hügli, Author & Economic Journalist

Journalist at financialmedia with a focus on economic and financial topics, in particular in the area of digital & crypto finance. Lecturer at the University of Applied Sciences in Business Administration Zurich (HWZ) on Bitcoin and blockchain. In addition, moderator and speaker at conferences and events.

Linkedin: https://www.linkedin.com/in/pascal-huegli

Yonghan Lee, Editor & Entrepreneur

Manager and entrepreneur in the field of blockchain, fintech, digital transformation and esports. Expert in portfolio & investment management and software development with many years of experience in the swiss banking sector and management consulting. Co-founder of the financial comic "The Bankey" as well as founder and CEO of Swiss Korean Blockchain Advisors, a consulting firm specialized in the Crypto Valley and the korean blockchain market.

Linkedin: https://www.linkedin.com/in/yonghanlee

Richard Dettling, Cartoonist & Banker, Investor

Risk, project and program manager in advisory and finance. Engaged in innovation in banking, fintech, digital transformation, portfolio & investment management, open banking, insurTech and real estate. In-depth knowledge and experience in financial and alternative investments. Founder of the financial comic "The Bankey".

Linkedin: https://www.linkedin.com/in/richard-dettling-ab59b3118

Printed in Poland
by Amazon Fulfillment
Poland Sp. z o.o., Wrocław

54230543R00130